PUBLIC SPEAKING

Public Speaking Secrets for Introverts on How to Influence People and Handle Small Talk With Confidence

(How to Be a Powerful, Dynamic and Confident Leader)

Tom Avery

Published by Rob Miles

© **Tom Avery**

All Rights Reserved

Charisma: Public Speaking Secrets for Introverts on How to Influence People and Handle Small Talk With Confidence (How to Be a Powerful, Dynamic and Confident Leader)

ISBN 978-1-989990-20-9

All rights reserved. No part of this guide may be reproduced in any form without permission in writing from the publisher except in the case of brief quotations embodied in critical articles or reviews.

Legal & Disclaimer

The information contained in this book is not designed to replace or take the place of any form of medicine or professional medical advice. The information in this book has been provided for educational and entertainment purposes only.

The information contained in this book has been compiled from sources deemed reliable, and it is accurate to the best of the Author's knowledge; however, the Author cannot guarantee its accuracy and validity and cannot be held liable for any errors or omissions. Changes are periodically made to this book. You must consult your doctor or get professional medical advice before using any of the suggested remedies, techniques, or information in this book.

Upon using the information contained in this book, you agree to hold harmless the Author from and against any damages, costs, and expenses, including any legal fees potentially resulting from the application of any of the information provided by this guide. This disclaimer applies to any damages or injury caused by the use and application, whether directly or indirectly, of any advice or information presented, whether for breach of contract, tort, negligence, personal injury, criminal intent, or under any other cause of action.

You agree to accept all risks of using the information presented inside this book. You need to consult a professional medical practitioner in order to ensure you are both able and healthy enough to participate in this program.

Table of Contents

INTRODUCTION 1

CHAPTER 1: SHARE PERSONAL ANECDOTES 4

CHAPTER 2: BREATHING 8

CHAPTER 3: NEVER TOO YOUNG, NEVER TOO OLD 18

CHAPTER 4: WHY WE FEAR PUBLIC SPEAKING 25

CHAPTER 5: CAUSES OF PUBLIC SPEAKING ANXIETY AND FEAR 30

CHAPTER 6: PARENTS- THEIR CHALLENGES 35

CHAPTER 7: SPEECH STRUCTURE. 39

CHAPTER 8: THE FEAR OF SPEAKING IN PUBLIC 52

CHAPTER 9: KNOW YOUR PURPOSE 58

CHAPTER 10: IT IS JUST TALKING 66

CHPTER 11: HOW TO OVERCOME YOUR FEAR OF PUBLIC SPEAKING 73

CHAPTER 12: THE OPEN 79

CHAPTER 13: SLAYING THE BEAST: HOW TO DEAL WITH THE FRIGHT 87

CHAPTER 14: OPENING OF THE SPEECH: START WITH A SPARK 97

CHAPTER 15: THE WHY 111

CHAPTER 16: UNDERSTANDING COMMUNICATION METHODS 113

CHAPTER 17: PRESENTATION 127

CHAPTER 18: TIPS BEFORE ENGAGING IN PUBLIC SPEAKING 143

CHAPTER 19: THE FIRST HONEY 146

CHAPTER 20: MAINTAIN A POSITIVE ATTITUDE 153

CHAPTER 21: PUBLIC SPEAKING IS EASY COMMUNICATION IS THE KEY 158

CHAPTER 22: SPEAK WITH MORE THAN YOUR VOICE 165

CHAPTER 23: HOW TO GIVE A DYNAMIC INTRODUCTION 176

CHAPTER 24: INFORMATIVE SPEAKING 181

CHAPTER 25: SHARPSHOOTERS AND HECKLERS 185

CONCLUSION 204

Introduction

Have you ever read a book that, even though it had a lot of good information in it, when you finished it you could not put it to practical use? Well, this book is not that kind of book. The secrets in this book can immediately be used to prepare you for speaking before a group of any size. It will even help you be prepared when speaking one on one with your superiors. This no doubt will help you in your advancement as you climb the ladder of success. If used correctly, it will be a sure confidence booster and money maker.

This book is about getting down to the practical means of preparation and execution of a speech. There are many books on the subject which deal with the technical side of the of public speaking. In this book, you will learn how to speak before an audience with ease and learn to be comfortable doing it.

Public speaking is not for the squeamish, it is a real challenge, but anyone who has the guts to do it, can do it. You can do it! Just follow these steps and you will find that you can become a successful speech maker.

I was one of the most frightened of any one I know when I first began to speak. But after implementing these techniques, I overcame my fears and now, over 5000 public speaking engagements later, I speak with ease. Yet, if you are a public speaker, you always know the importance of being fresh and innovative in your presentation. It is a continual growth process and will be as long as you speak to groups of people.

There are many types of speaking that you may need to use throughout your life. You may use informative speaking to inform your audience about a topic. A persuasive speech can be used to change your audience's beliefs or actions. A commemorative speech is often used to honor or remember a person or event. A eulogy is a good example of a commemorative speech. An introduction speech is used to introduce the main speaker to the audience. An acceptance speech is used to accept an award, gift, or another type of public recognition.

No matter what type of speech you perform, these secrets will reveal to you how to be an excellent public speaker.

Chapter 1: Share Personal Anecdotes

Have you ever been to a live show or performance in which those on stage did not really interact with you, or open up to you?
Many live performers or speakers can engage with the material they are delivering, and deliver it well at face value.
It is another skill altogether to share a personal anecdote, as you would a friend or family member, but this can make all the difference. The most effective speakers and performers I have seen at engaging the audience are often those who make a point of sharing the backstory of what they are presenting, and explain why the material they are delivering is important to them.
In the case of poets or singer-songwriters, sharing anecdotes or stories can provide the audience with information that adds another layer of meaning and depth to a poem or song they already knew and

loved, but which they may have never fully understood. It could also add more of a human touch to something they may be hearing for the first time, making them more likely to pay attention and take something meaningful away from it, as opposed to simply turning their pages or tuning their guitar strings in silence.

Otherwise, a much higher number of the audience may be inclined to check their phones or social media or talk amongst themselves. I was once at a live show in Kentish Town, London, where the band just launched into their final track without introducing it verbally. A girl next to me was simply sat there reading a book by torchlight, and when this track began, she did not look up or react in any way.

Stand-up comedians are often most effective when using extended anecdotes based on personal experience, as opposed to simply reeling off an endless stream of one-liners. One-liners can be great in moderation, but rely too heavily on them, and the performer risks their set appearing forced, overly slick or superficial.

Motivational speakers are often most effective when sharing their own personal 'rags to riches' stories (and I'm not just referring to material riches). This is in contrast to those who simply spout messages without really giving a reason as to why people should take their word for it. Without anecdotal evidence, the audience could be thinking 'This is great, but how do I know this stuff works?'

One evening, I had the role of timing other people's speeches. I had to give a short introductory speech explaining my role, and the importance of time-management in general. As part of this, I told a story about an open-mic night I once performed at which was less strict in this regard, due to there not being a full bill of acts, and told how the compere had joked about time being an abstract concept.

If speakers tell their own story, it can give their advice more power, and give the audience more incentive to listen. It can also make the audience feel more compelled to share some of their own relevant experiences, if there is an opportunity for them to raise their hands and make comments in this way.

Chapter 2: Breathing

Breathing Better

Most people don't think about breathing. Well, I suppose when you do something 25,000 times a day the novelty is bound to wear off at some point. Learning how to breathe better however is the first step to getting a grounded, confident sounding voice that will allow you to deliver speeches that a world leader would be proud of!

Breathing properly can help calm your nerves before speaking, and can support you all the way through to delivering your final statement. It takes practice and patience, but the exercises in this section can help you to breathe more deeply (which has a calming effect), increase your lung capacity (which allows you to speak for longer in a single breath), and maintain a good breathing pattern (which helps to maintain rhythm and pace).

Finding the Diaphragm

Breathing starts from your diaphragm, which is a sheet of muscle underneath your lungs. The diaphragm lowers as you breathe in, pulling the air down into your lungs, and rises as you breathe out, forcing the air back up and out. Most of us in our everyday lives ignore the diaphragm and breathe mostly from the top of our lungs using our upper chests. This restricts us to using only about 40% of our total lung capacity. Our lungs evolved by natural selection to supply the body with enough oxygen needed to hunt for food and survive in harsh conditions, but as our lives are much more pedestrian today, we rarely use them to their full potential.

By exercising the diaphragm we can unlock the unused 60% and boost our speaking potential by taking full advantage of the set of lungs evolution has given us. The first 3 exercises in this section will show you how to find and exercise your diaphragm.

1. The Full Breath

Begin this exercise simply by standing with your back straight and your arms relaxed:

Place a hand over your belly button and feel as you breathe in and out. If your stomach only rises very slightly as you breathe in, it's likely that you're breathing too much from your upper chest.

On your next in-breath, force your stomach out and actively try to breathe deeper down, filling your lungs from the bottom up. This can take a while for some people to grow accustomed to, as they are so used to taking short breaths.

Keep breathing this way, in through your nose and out through your mouth, and try to slow your breathing tempo down.

You don't have to breathe like this all the time (although it wouldn't hurt, for actors and most athletes it's second nature), but if you remember to breathe from your stomach when the nerves kick in as you prepare to speak, and keep it going until you can rest, it will go a long way to calming you and grounding your voice.

2. Panting Sequence

This exercise requires you to breathe quickly from your diaphragm. Simply pant quickly, taking sharp breaths between each cycle, and keep a hand on your stomach to ensure you're pushing from the diaphragm:

Begin with 24 short breaths, panting on each out-breath and snatching a quick in-breath between each pant:

Move on to panting twice for each out-breath, for a total of 48 times in the sequence.

Next begin panting three times for each in-breath, so for 24 in-breaths pant 72 times.

3. Intoned Panting

This exercise is simply a voiced version of Panting in sequence.

Begin with 24 short breaths, intoning a 'huh' sound for each:

Move on to intoning 'huh' twice for each out-breath, for a total of 48 times in the sequence.

Finally begin intoning 'huh' three times for each in-breath, so for 24 in-breaths pant 72 times.

You should be able to feel the diaphragm working hard in these exercises, and if done correctly it can be quite tiring, making your stomach feel like you've performed a set of sit-ups.

Lung Capacity

Now that you know how to use a larger proportion of your lungs, and how to push from your diaphragm with force, you can move on to increasing the maximum amount of air you can hold in them. Increasing your lung capacity will allow you to speak for longer periods of time before having to take a breath. This leads to better pacing, a more controlled rhythm of speaking and allows you to experiment with words and say them with more of an impact.

Divers and swimmers naturally have greater lung capacities as they are used to holding their breath for a long period of time, and actors and opera singers have to learn this skill to be able to perform with greater ease and endurance. Although you may not be a diver or an opera singer, you can still benefit from increasing your lung capacity, both for public speaking and for general health reasons.

As an example, try to say the following sentence in one single out-breath. Speak at your natural pace and volume, pause for commas but don't breathe in, and see how far you get:

The lawyer, having convinced his client to plead guilty, was now faced with the problem of avoiding the revelation of his own part in the criminal act, a lapse in judgment that, while done with the best of intentions, was nonetheless a violation of his oath as an attorney, a violation that might conceivably result in his disbarment, indictment, and even imprisonment.

How far did you get? Most people wouldn't be able to get to the end in one single breath, so don't worry if you couldn't. Try out the rest of the exercises in this section and keep coming back to read the sentence again, you should see some improvement. Even if you did manage it, you'll find that after increasing your lung capacity it will become much easier.

4. Lung Capacity Test

Before each step of this exercise take one full in-breath, and complete the step on your out-breath. Speak clearly and accurately and try to empty your lungs by the end of the phrase (take note of the target you have to aim for and try to release the air proportionately. Don't cheat and take in-breaths before the end of the phrase, if you can't finish just start again:

Recite the numbers 1 to 10.
Recite the numbers 1 to 15.
Recite the numbers 1 to 25.

Recite numbers for as long as you can before you need to breathe in. Make a note of how far you get as it should increase with practice.

Recite the days of the week from Monday to Sunday.

Recite the days of two weeks.

Recite the days of three weeks.

Recite the months of the year.

Recite the months of two years.

5. Holding the Breath

A good way to increase your lung capacity is simply to practice holding your breath. Practicing this regularly will allow you to increase your tolerance threshold and also allow you to hold more air in your lungs over a longer period of time.

Simply take a full breath in and hold for as long as you comfortably can. DO NOT hold for too long for obvious reasons, if you feel dizzy or faint return to your regular breathing pattern.

Release the breath in one of the ways described in the next two exercises.

6. Low Hum

After holding your breath, instead of releasing the air normally and taking a quick relief in-breath, release the air slowly whilst making a humming noise at the lowest pitch you can reach.

Of course breathe in when you need to, but try to keep the hum going for as long as possible. This will increase your lung capacity and your endurance over time, and is also a good way to add a warm quality to your voice.

7. Quick Release

Again, begin by holding a full breath. This time, instead of releasing the air slowly, breathe it out as fast as you can, and then take a second full breath in and hold. Repeat this sequence 8 times.

This exercise will get you used to taking quick breaths, which can be helpful when delivering speeches and useful for keeping momentum in a debate. If you begin to feel dizzy, be sure to stop the exercise. It's important to learn your body's limits, and practicing these exercises will help you to know those limits and, over time, to increase them.

Chapter 3: Never Too Young, Never Too Old

Whoever said that old dogs can't learn new tricks is a very unfortunate person. He or she was locked with a wrong belief about age. Personally, I'd rather entertain the saying that age is only a number for a million reasons. For one, age is definitely just a number. Nowadays, age has little to do with the accomplishment that one may have. You could be fourteen and become a world wide singing sensation – or a model perhaps. Mark Zuckerberg, the father of Facebook, is one of the self made millionaires under 30 that the world has seen recently. Who's not on Facebook right? This guy has changed how people connect across the globe. Now it would be safe to say that sheer talent, dedication and persistence can definitely get you a long way. Adults who exemplify the same principles are worthy of mention as well. Across the globe, people who are well beyond their years are not weighed down by their age. We've heard of people in their 60's or 70's who go back to school or finish a law degree to complete the fulfilment of their lives.

As a people, we've come a long way from the time that everything was strictly dictated by the society; a time when children are supposed to be happy, jolly kids while adults become stiff, responsible individuals.Things are way different now. With technologies and a growing borderless international community, anyone can be whoever they want to be at any age.

Speaking to an audience is a universal fear that affects both young and grown people. And facing your fears head on is the only way to overcome this. So whether you're a teenager or an accomplished individual, here are some of the things that you can gain in enhancing your public speaking skills at any point in your life.

- Earn the respect and admiration of people you interact with
- Give informative presentations and reports that are lively and creative
- Project yourself better with overflowing confidence
- Maximize the power of words to heal, inspire or promote change as you will
- Expressing your concerns effectively can help build any relationship
- Go about life limitless – any fear or obstacle will be insignificant to you since you've overcome the biggest challenge of public speaking
- Enjoy a number of opportunities to improve yourself and others

These are only a few of the things that you can expect when you take the first step in brushing up your public communication skills. Everyone can benefit from learning how to handle and overcome the fear of talking in front of a large crowd. Though starting young gives one more time to enjoy the benefits and reap the rewards of this valuable social skill, that setback should not discourage anyone from fulfilling their desire of being a confident and influential speaker.After all, life is what you make it. Take the first step or lead your kids to take theirs towards a life of confidence and success.

The Number One Fear? Really?

Being scared is a wonderful feeling. It may not be at all that positive or pleasant that feeling it is a nice way to remind oneself of being human and all our flaws, needs and desires that come with it. In the face of fear, each of us is presented with challenges that can either make or break us. Of course, whatever route we take is highly dependent of the choices and actions that we decide to follow. Fear is nothing but normal – it is what we do with that fear that makes a whole lot of difference in our lives.

Many people around the globe will gladly choose to die rather than stand in front of a crowd to deliver a message or a speech.

It may go as mild as having sweaty palms or shaky hands but it may also go as extreme as not being able to move or say a word in front of everyone. A Texas University Study in 2006 showed that the fear of public speaking affects people in varying degrees. Some people may be stricken with anxiety only during the actual preparations as others get the same feeling all throughout – from the preparation up until the presentation ends. Though it is not necessarily a bad thing, uncontrollable speech anxiety can be of a great cost.

Fear of public speaking or glossophobia is quite common as it affects 75% of the population. Though everyone may suffer a certain degree of anxiety when faced with the challenge to be in the spotlight, excessive fear of it that may cause troubles in school, work, social gatherings or relationships may be a truthful manifestation of this shared difficulty.

This social phobia does not explicitly exhibit itself at all times. It may happen that a person who may be having this difficulty can dance and sing in front of a crowd provided that saying a word is not mandatory. Stage fright such as this does not only occur in formal speaking engagements since majority of careers entails presentations and interactions with other people. When left without much attention, glossophobia can lead to losing one's job, shattered relationships and depression among others.

Though this condition is a tad more difficult to prevent than medical situations, treatment and elimination of this phobia is very possible. Cognitive-behavioral therapy is one of the most common ways to defeat stage fright. This method teaches individuals to foster a positive self-talk when faced with fear. Moreover, relaxation techniques are also thought to allow for a better handling of panic attacks. In some cases, medications are prescribed by doctors or therapists to aid in the treatment process. One may also opt to attend public speaking courses or seminars if undergoing medical treatments is a little overboard since it is possible that an individual only needs a little support and encouragement to defeat the fear.

Fear of the unknown as well as that of rejection greatly affects glossophibia. Freeing oneself from one's limiting cause can only be resolved by understanding your needs and what causes it. Once done, you can begin reclaiming your life and lead it to a better state. Your success begins by not being a part of the statistic anymore.

Chapter 4: Why We Fear Public Speaking

Teachers and professors, almost in every course, require students to present on a topic. These assignments, although dreadful to students, are aimed at preparing students for the job market, e.g., to hold their ground and succeed in interviews with potential employers.

I remember as a university student hearing other classmates sigh when professors required students to present at least once in the classroom. Speaking publicly is very unpopular, but I want to help you avoid what happened to me. I want to help you develop the courage to speak in front of others and to not allow such fear to control you. It is a crucial skill we need, and I want to help you develop it.

To even begin to lay out what worked for me to overcome my fear of speaking in front of people, we first have to attempt to articulate why it is that we fear doing it. There are some obvious reasons why we do: 1.) we don't want to look stupid in front of others; 2.) we are worried about what others will say about us; and 3.) we just feel uncomfortable being in the spotlight. I believe our fear grips us deeper. I believe there is another reason, hard to identify , that causes us to fear speaking publicly--and it has a lot to do with our background and upbringing.

To illustrate, I was raised by both of my parents and three of my siblings—one sister and two brothers. We were not a dysfunctional family, nor were we a very close one. My brothers were always willing to lend me a hand, and I was to them, but we didn't share our most personal secrets with each other. Informal, invisible boundaries existed and not one of us felt comfortable crossing them.

That said, my brothers were fun to be around with. Their humor, however, was always very cruel. Not to say they weren't and aren't funny, they were and still are. They still make me laugh uncontrollably, but, unfortunately, it is at the expense of others. My brothers were harsh to almost everyone outside of our immediate family. They constantly and rigorously criticized everyone we met, from their way of being to their physical characteristics. This cruel humor exhibited by my brothers subconsciously affected the way I behaved in front of others. I didn't know it, until my second year of college.

One Sunday afternoon, as I sat outside in my old, wooden rocking chair underneath my porch, I started putting the pieces together and I realized my brothers played a major role in how I conducted myself in front of others. Growing up with two brothers who criticized anyone who wasn't like them exposed me to an unhealthy environment. Unconsciously, without realizing it, I assumed those around me were like my brothers—persons who enjoyed bringing others down. Thus, I was very careful with what I said and what I did in front of others, as I was in front of my brothers. This was the initial stage of developing a fear of speaking confidently in front of others. Whenever I spoke in front of people, I felt as if my brothers were present and were ready to gun at me with criticisms. Eventually, keeping my guard up most of the time, trying my best not to sound or act stupidly, led to a full-blown fear of public speaking. I frequently caught myself thinking too much about what to say and how to act.

I'm using my background to make some sense of the fear I experienced. Now, ask yourself, do you have anybody close to you who is hostile to others that affects the way you believe others perceive you? If you don't, are you the hostile person who criticizes others and believe others will criticize you if they get the chance? If we do, we allow ourselves to construct a negative view of our peers, thinking they will certainly think badly of us just like we think badly of them. But most people are not like that. People are genuine and naturally good persons. If you have someone who affects the way you interact with others, remember, not everyone is like that person. And if it is you who is being harmful to others, not everyone is like you. Perhaps we need to reflect on our character, change it if hostile, to let the healing begin. This allows us to trust our peers more, to feel safe enough to express our true selves around them.

So, sit back, relax, and think deeply about what is potentially contributing to the anxiety and fear you have of interacting with large groups of people. Once you figure it out, most likely without precision (you'll only have a general idea of what contributes to your fear), try to work on eliminating that contributor. It is the initial step we must take to take control of our anxiety, liberate ourselves, and start enjoying school and life without our most pressing fear.

Chapter 5: Causes Of Public Speaking Anxiety And Fear

To understand your fear or anxiety of public speaking, you must first know what caused it in the first place. Was it a traumatic incident in school? Or was your self-confidence squashed at home or at work? Whatever the reason is, you must learn about it, and then use the knowledge you gained to conquer your fears of speaking in front of a crowd. Below is a list of common causes of public speaking anxiety and fears.

Repeated traumatic incidents regarding speaking and self-expression.

Some people experience traumatic incidents during their childhood that represses their ability to speak and be heard. These incidents are usually taken for granted, or are overlooked as normal events in a child's life. However, if such incidents are repeated, then the trauma makes the child's self-confidence wane, and this is what he or she remembers while growing up.

Consider the following example:

Bobby is not a great speaker, but he is intent on becoming one. At the age of six, Bobby joined a speech competition in his school. He practiced day and night for that competition, and wanted to win first place badly. However, Gary, the class bully, had also signed up for the competition. To intimidate Bobby, Gary teased and taunted him every day saying that Bobby was going to forget his speech and make a fool of himself in front of the whole school. Gary made sure that Bobby felt discouraged and bullied every day. The teachers never caught Gary making fun of Bobby and if they did, they did not do enough to repair the damage Gary was slowly inflicting on Bobby.

On the day of the competition, Bobby was nervous. He tried to remember what his parents had said about staying calm, but all he could focus on was how Gary had teased and taunted him. When it was his turn to go up the stage, Bobby was sweating excessively. He was able to deliver the first part of his speech without any mistake, but then in the middle of his speech, he remembered how Gary had bullied him for the past few days. He suddenly forgot all that he had rehearsed, and started stuttering. At first there was a small ripple of laughter from the crowd, and then the teachers tried to hush the students, but failed miserably. The entire school assembly laughed out loud because poor Bobby was stuttering and having difficulty finishing his speech.

Now, note how Gary's repeated actions made such an impact on Bobby's speech. If Gary had not repeated his taunts and teases, Bobby would probably have made it through his speech just fine. However, since he was subjected to repeated traumatic incidents directly related to speaking, Bobby grew up thinking that he would never be good enough to be a public speaker. That failure, catalyzed by Gary's taunts and Bobby's response to them, cemented Bobby's fear of—not public speaking, though he certainly thought that's what it was—but the fear of failing and making a fool of himself.

If you have any similar experiences to what Bobby went through, then chances are high that those experiences are what triggered your anxieties and fears of public speaking in the first place.

Minimal to no socialization

Kids who do not have enough time or opportunities to socialize usually grow up to be shy. Because they lack experience interacting with their peers or other people, they tend to be naturally anxious about having to speak out in public.

If you did not have many friends as a child, or if your contact with your peers and neighbors was severely limited, then that may be the cause of your public-speaking anxiety. You are not used to being put in front of others to speak your mind, so your body tries to cope with this stressful situation by releasing adrenaline and sweat, as well as making you shake out of nervousness.

Pessimism

As much as public speaking fears can be caused by external and environmental factors, so too can they be caused by internal factors such as pessimism and consistent negative self-talk. Whether you are an adult, teen, or child hardly makes a difference. If you are prone to making yourself feel bad, or if you continually discourage yourself, then your fears of public speaking are self-inflicted. People who keep thinking that they will make a fool of themselves, or that they will forget their speeches or that they simply cannot do it, are more likely to fail at public speaking than people who choose to keep a positive outlook.

Chapter 6:Parents- Their Challenges

I am sure that after reading the incident in chapter 1, you would be tempted to try out the same with your kids too. But before you succumb to this temptation, let us first try to understand why you should invest in extra effort with your kids on this skill especially when you send them to the best of the schools.

Reason no. 1

Time spent in school

Out of the 24 hrs./day, a student spends approximately 6 hours in school, which means that a student spends 75% of the time at home with his family members. School has a lot of influence on the personality of the child, but the family plays a significant role too. Parents can facilitate the children to develop, grow and take them to the next ●♏✷♏● ♌◆✦ the children must develop their capability to do the work on their own.

Reason no. 2

Shortcuts

Some parents only focus on the academics which means getting good marks and nothing else. Many parents are even happy when their child crams everything and secures a good grade. There are parents who select only that tuition teacher for their child, who gives notes rather than those who wish to develop the child and take them to the next level. Such students later face a lot of internal struggle later when it comes to speaking in Public.

Reason no. 3

Students of International Level Schools

I have met students from international level schools who have confessed that whenever they have tried to stand and speak in the class, their class mates laugh at them, so they choose to take separate coaching for themselves. They hesitate because the world only shuts their mouth and does not let them speak. Their world is exceedingly small which includes their friends and class mates.

Reason no. 4

Fear

There are others in the class who just do not speak up out of the fear of ridicule. You need to figure out if your child is amongst them and you as a parent should give child a support to fight the world.

Reason no. 5

Fun Time

Many parents consciously want their child to acquire this skill. One of my friends confessed that he went to the best of the convent schools. The school excelled not only in studies but extra-curricular activities as well. He had every opportunity to become a good public speaker, but he and his group of friends were unmindful to its benefit and future impact. Once the professional life started, he realised his mistake but just could not get enough time to work on it. He is 45yrs.

old and has started working on his skills now.

Chapter 7: Speech Structure.

The structure of the speech means simply how the speech is laid out. It is imperative that you have a structure in place as an unprepared speaker is a broke one!

I've seen many failed sales presentations just because the speaker didn't have any direction to his speech, he mumbled his way through leaving it up to chance and the audience wasn't too impressed and neither was the promoter who flew him interstate just to be there that day. Nobody won that day, and that speaker probably won't get a gig in that town again. So make sure you have a solid structure to your speech.

Although there are several different kinds of structures that you can use, I've found that the easiest and most effective is to have an opening, a body of the speech, and a conclusion. Sound familiar yes? It's worked for every other speaker that existed and still works now. When you follow this structure the audience always knows the direction you're heading to and they're not confused. You could imagine a very confused audience when you approach the stage and start giving the body of your speech, then 30 minutes in your decide tointroduce yourselfand mention your credibility, and then you close your speech ... this would be very confusing indeed and would sound absolutely ludicrous.

Opening

Introducing yourself on stage is not as difficult as you might think. There is usually a host who will begin the introductions, then you finish where he left

off. It always builds more value and "social proof" if a speaker introduces you

and mentions your credentials rather than you jumping up on the stage in front of a "cold" audience, nobody knowing who you are! They won't trust or buy from you unless you spend a lot of time "warming" them up by explaining why they should listen to you. You can even do your own introduction in fact I've done this many times before when I ran seminars interstate and was low on staff.

It can be as simple as ...

"Hi everyone my name is Alex and you may have heard of me on radio or seen some of my videos online teaching speaker training. For the last 4 years I've been coaching many entrepreneurs, business owners and sales people how to build a million dollar speaking business from scratch ..."

I found the best ways to "warm" up an audience is to tell your story on how you got to be where you are today, everyone loves stories **especially rags to riches stories**, the idea is to first get them to trust you by relating to them and making them realize that YOU used to be one of them, you WERE suffering from their same problems, then explain some of those problems while bringing up the pain they must be feeling and then provide them with the answer to their problems.

Using a humorous story about yourself, your family, or something funny about where you live is one of the easiest and most effective ways to grab the audiences' attention also. It gives the audience a little insight into who you are and helps them to feel more comfortable.

Nobody likes a speaker who rattles on about how elegant their wealthy lifestyle is and how perfect

they are. Here's a newsflash for you ... people inherently dislike perfect

people. Only when you have faults, make mistakes and manage your slip

ups people realize that you are human after all and you are just like them, this is the first step to building trust. **Admit you are not perfect**.

Your speech needs a strong opening that gets the audiences attention. It has to hook them immediately. Making a strong opening is an essential skill for a public speaker. If you don't have them from the get go then you won't have them at all its just that simple. Many speakers start their opening by thanking the promoters, talking about the hotel, mentioning the helpful staff who organized the room. Hers another fact for you ... **the audience doesn't care!** They want an answer to their problems and if you can't relate to their problems quick smart then you'll lose their interest quick smart.

Have you ever been watching channels on your home TV and started flipping the channel? Wows there are a lot of channels to choose from aren't there now? Well most people spend on average about 2-3 seconds per channel before they flip it over, and then flip it again ... only 3 seconds to decide whether or not they are going to watch that channel or flip it over to another... the same principle sadly applies to speaking. Within the first 5 seconds you have to CAPTURE the audiences attention and imagination by telling a gripping story, telling a funny joke, or giving an introduction that will entertain and inspire them to listen to you. Here's an example of a strong opening for a serious subject. Below it are the techniques that were used to craft it into a gut-wrenching, attention grabbing opening.

"Tobacco..............Alcohol................Guns...................Items used by criminals that were captured....from a child at a middle school."

This opening uses several techniques that are extremely effective when opening a speech.

Drama - drama builds by pausing after every single word.This increases the tension.It also magnifies the intensity of the topic you're talking about.

Misdirection - misdirection in the ending sentence explains the importance of the three previous words.You lead the audience into thinking that the items mentioned belong to a criminal, and then let them know they were a child's. A complete contrast from what the audience is thinking.

Alliteration - the use of one letter for several words in a sentence. Criminals, captured, child. This poetic use of language makes a striking statement.

Mid-sentence pause after 'captured' signals the audience that you're going to make an important statement. This intensifies the previous statements and allows the audience to dwell on what you said, this also adds importance to

what you said (the perception of importance)

All the tension, danger, and drama that put the audience on the edge of their seats are completed with 16 words. Any opening that has these points will be a STRONG opening.

If you quotes facts and figures as an opener you'll give good, solid information, but you'll be as boring as a box of rocks. A strong opening may shock, anger, bring the audience to tears, or make them laugh. But they must **FEEL** something. That feeling is what you build upon for the rest of your speech.

If your audience cant FEEL what you're saying then no emotional connection is made. The audience and you will be two distinct entities completely un- correlated from each other. They wont be emotionally engaged in your

stories and thus the impact it was intending to be delivered wont be delivered

and all will be lost.

Body

The body of the speech is where you present what you want the audience to learn, become aware, motivate; whatever point you want to get across. This is where you give data; stories and quotes inspire and motivate your audience.

The obvious reason why you give your content after you've introduced yourself

properly as opposed to just jumping in there and just giving valuable content is quite simply if people don't know who you are, what you're going to be revealing in your talk and why they should listen to you (must show them your credibility) then they wont be emotionally around to listen to the "body"
of the speech.

Keeping the audiences attention is essential if you want to get your points across.You've begun to build a rapport with them in the opening.Continue to build upon that by following with pertinent information they can use.

You've just brought them through a lot of emotion in the opening.Give them something that will help it be absorbed; information that will bring your points home.

Use different techniques to keep the flow in the body of the speech moving.

Quotes will add weight and credibility. They make your points time-tested truths.

It also shows you have researched your material and are well prepared.

Stories take the audience through a sequence of events that underscores your points. Its always better to use true stories but if you are lacking them then "borrow" them. Stories are an emotional tool to engage an audience. The best speakers in the world are avid storytellers and can captivate an

audience in a heartbeat. The take the audience on an emotional rollercoaster filled with heart warming stories, stories of sorrow, inspiration, courage, sadness and fulfillment. Some of the most provoking stories are those of sadness which brings an audience to tears.

Props visually illustrate the points you are making. These are always very welcomed if there are too many facts and statistics, your audience will

probably want a change and a prop would be much appreciated.

Magic tricks are special props. By using magic tricks, you can sink a point into their brains because every time they think of the magic trick, they'll think of the point that went with it. This is very similar to props and can hold audiences attention easily. However it's important you **don't use too many magic tricks** and become an "entertainer", otherwise you'll lose your authority and you won't be taken seriously.

Changing the pace of the speech. When you want to make the audience sit up and pay attention you speak rapidly and forcefully. When you want them to absorb what you've just said, you slow your speech down, and lower the tone of your voice. Your tone of your voice will set the mood for your presentation. Practice lowering your tone and deepening your voice, speak slower as these techniques will command more authority as opposed to speaking fast in a high pitched voice.

Pausing just before and/or just after an essential point will make that point stand out.Doing this two times in succession, with you voice slightly raised the second time, is like an underline and an exclamation mark at the end of a sentence.

The body is where you do the largest portion of your teaching, illustrating, informing, and inspiring. Whatever topic your speech is about, this is where you give everything to focus and motivate your audience.

Notes on selling to your audience:

If you plan on selling your product or service to the audience hence as we call it a sales presentation then you need to mention your product several

times during your body, DON'T try to sell it in the body just mention it and move on.

Most speakers who fail miserably at the close make the mistake of not even mentioning their product during their talk and when the time comes to close the deal at the end they mention their product or service and the audience wonders "where did that come from". I constantly mention the fact I've run coaching programs around Australia, I mention the amounts I charge customers and by doing this it reminds them that coaching is an option if they want to further their education on their speaking skills. Then at the end of my presentation I'll sell my coaching programs and to my surprise it's a lot easier when it's done this way because they are "open" to the idea now.

Chapter 8: The Fear Of Speaking In Public

Has this ever happened to you? Whenever you walk onto a stage and your mind is racing at 200 mph with your clammy hands tightly grasp to a small piece of paper, followed by the excessive amount of sweat pouring out of your palms, and but once you open your mouth and try to speak, no words came out, because your throat closed completely shut. If yes, then you are in the not-so-happy world of glossophobia, also known as the fear of public speaking.

Having a fear of public speaking is one of the most prevalent of all phobias; it even trumps the fear of death. So, if you think that you would rather die instead of speaking in front of an audience, you are not alone.

What is Glossophobia?

Contrary to what most people believe, the fear of public speaking is not limited to just giving speeches. Glossophobia is severe anxiety that people get when trying to talk to any number of people. It means a glossophobe gets the jitters even when obligated to speak in front of an audience, regardless of the number of people involved.

Unlike most phobias, almost everyone is fearful of speaking in public, the severity of the anxiety attacks is the only thing that is different in most cases. For instance, most students secretly pray that their teachers would not call them out to recite in front of the class, especially on a topic that they are not comfortable with or prepared. Even seasoned performers get butterflies in their stomachs before every show; they would be lying if they say otherwise.

Here is a couple of famous people who suffered from fear of public speaking (the key word here is "suffered"):

Bruce Willis – Detective John McClane may not have any qualms about taking on an entire cell of terrorists by himself, but he was actually quite a shy, stuttering kid. Bruce Willis once had an uncontrollable stutter, which was the reason he hated giving speeches or even just reciting in front of his class. Fortunately, with the help of a speech therapist, he was able to speak normally and confidently, and along with his speech impediment, his fear of public speaking went away as well.

Rowan Atkinson – The "Man with a Rubber Face" also has a speech impediment, particularly with pronouncing the letter "B", which made him fearful of speaking in front of a crowd. Instead of being ashamed of his speech impediment, Rowan Atkinson learned how to use it as a tool for his comedic performances; now, he has become one of the most well-known actors in the showbiz industry.

Samuel L. Jackson – This may come as a surprise to many, but the always-eloquent Mr. Jackson once was afraid of speaking in public because he had a stutter. Thanks to his speech therapist's goading to join an acting class, we are now able to enjoy the many different iconic film characters played by Samuel L. Jackson.

Now, if everyone is afraid of speaking in public (to a certain degree), why do most people seem comfortable when delivering talks, speeches, monologues, and the like? It's because they know how to harness the power of their fear and use it against itself, and the good news here is that you can learn how to do it as well.

Why do People Hate Giving Speeches?

Okay, the word "hate" may be too much to describe the feeling that people with a fear of public speaking has, but if you ask them anything about it, they will tell you that they really do hate talking in front of other people. What is really going through your head when you learn that you have to give a speech? Do you really hate giving speeches, or are you just afraid of making a fool of yourself?

One of the reasons why people dread giving speeches is because they are afraid of the stares of the audience. Most people are afraid that once they step on the stage, the audience will judge every move they make, and this makes them extremely anxious. It will often lead to them overcompensating due to their insecurities, which in turn makes them even more nervous; it's a never-ending and a vicious cycle.

However, if you dislike making speeches because you feel like they are an inconvenience then you might not be suffering from the fear of public speaking at all, and that you genuinely do hate speaking in front of a crowd. Cases like this are rare, and nowadays, if you really desire to move forward in your life and career, you must be able to address at least a small audience.

A few words before you continue...

Okay, so ultimately beating a phobia will require you to get help from a professional therapist, but you can still do something to at lessen your fears at the very least. No one can claim they are entirely free of their phobia; chances are there will still be some traces of your fear left after extensive therapy. Aiming for the impossible is one surefire way to disappointment. For now, be realistic with your goals, and give yourself a workable timeline to complete them.

Chapter 9: Know Your Purpose

Before you step your feet in front of a huge crowd with a big head light spotted on you, you should have first and foremost known the reason of your presence there.

Ask yourself, "Why? Why am I standing here?"

What Is My Purpose?

Defining your purpose determines your role and at the same time provides you a grasp of what you would like to achieve once you started to face an audience whose primary intention is to listen to every word that you deliver. Your purpose, which is considered as your presentation's backbone, serves as your guide on how you would present your piece.

An oral presentation is far too different from a **GOOD** oral presentation. One is considered good if it conveys effective communication between the speaker which is you, and the receiver which is the audience you are trying to speak to. **Your**

main purpose is to communicate. Without effective communication, you can imagine yourself wastefully talking to a brick of wall.

Remember that it is not just the way you present your piece that matters, it is also about how your audience understands and receives your messages to them.

Your basic objectives are always directed on increasing the knowledge of your audience about the certain topic you are discussing, increasing their understanding of what you are trying to imply, and if possible, encourage a new way of thinking or a change in behavior.

Ask yourself these examples of basic questions:

What type of approach should I use?
What are the necessary things that they need to know?
Will I entertain them?
How will I entertain them?
Do I need to impress them?
How will I present myself in the most

impressive way possible?

Do I need something from them?
If I do need something from them, how will I earn it?
Do I need to inspire them?
What will be the proper words to tell in order to inspire them?
Should I persuade them?
How can I visually show my purpose?
Who am I going to talk to?
What is their level of thinking?
What approach should I use with this type of audience?
What interests this audience?
What outcome do I want to achieve?
For how long should I present my talk?
The list is endless. You should not only limit yourself to these questions. You will certainly have other things to consider once you have figured out what you want to achieve. These questions will serve as a ladder towards your main goal.

This purpose would be achieved once the subsequent guides are successfully done. Once you already know what your purpose is, then you are ready to take the succeeding steps.

Words to Ponder

Be it in a form of lecture where you are expected to impart knowledge on the most interesting and informative things possible within a limited time, in a form of sugary persuasion to win a group of people's valuable "yes," in a form of a motivational speech to inspire people to initiate a new change, or just merely in a form of entertainment by catching your audience's tickle bone, it is always important to cover only the essentials and disregard the unnecessary. By doing this, you have to limit your presentation only within the scope of your purpose. And this purpose is realistically patterned according to your audience needs and expectations.

A Sound Body, A Sound Mind

Have you ever felt like there are butterflies

existing in your stomach as the upcoming presentation is nearly approaching? Have you ever felt like your tongue is tied making you to stutter the words slipping at the back of your mind at the middle of your speech? Or have you ever felt so restless that your heart un-calmly beats on the fastest rate than it ever did 5 minutes before your turn on the spotlight?

Well, those are just normal physiological reactions. These are the manifestations of how your body reacts to the stress you are facing. These physiologic feelings may be distracting, but this chapter will help you know how to control these.

Hakuna Matata Exercises

From the name itself, "Hakuna Matata" means no worries. These exercises will aid you to overcome those tensions within your nerves. It helps you to physically and mentally calm yourself down to avoid those jittery-heart-racing-stuttering presentation experiences.

Deep Breathing exercises

There are numerous ways on how to breathe deeply. But basically, it is about prolonging the inhalation and exhalation of air to facilitate better and adequate ventilation. Start by choosing a peaceful and quiet place conducive for relaxation. Find your most comfortable position. I suggest sitting on your chair with your back straight. Rest your arms on your lap or put them on your stomach. Inhale through your nose slowly for 5 seconds. Hold your breath for 3 seconds, then slowly exhale air through your mouth for 7 seconds. Repeat this 10-20 times.

Progressive Muscle Relaxation

Human body and mind are connected in a way we barely understand. Applying tension-relaxation to your muscles may result to having a peaceful mind. With one muscle at a time, gradually start the tension at your feet, and gradually work your way up to your face. In the end, expect that you will be more relieved and your muscles will be more relaxed.

Guided Imagery

This would require your imagination. It involves putting yourself within a scene in which you find very soothing and calming. Gently close your eyes and explore what your mind has to show.It can be a scene of you with your loved ones walking along the beach during a bright sunny day, or a social gathering you have always been excited to think of, or relatively see yourself standing in front of a huge audience applauding for a good presentation. You can do this in conjunction with a relaxing music often used for meditation.

Words to Ponder

I bet you know how distressing a day would be if it is preceded by a not-so-good-complete-hours of sleep. One factor why people feel anxious and nervous before an oral presentation is because of lack of sleep. You feel tired and your eyelids cannot help but droop slowly until it closes completely, and you tend to have that strong attraction to your ever-beloved bed. It would make focusing harder and there is an increased chance that you'd forget what you have prepared. Therefore, always remember that sleep is an essential preparation for your big day.

Make sure that you have adequately consumed a good meal. Studies showed that an empty stomach can aggravate your anxiety and nervousness. Settle first your bathroom rituals to ensure that your gastrointestinal function is good and reacts accordingly to you.

Chapter 10: It Is Just Talking

Some people are born speakers. Most are not. Hence, you are not alone when you say that you do not enjoy making speeches and speaking in front of a large audience. Stage fright is inevitable. Actors are always nervous to a certain degree before every play.

Perhaps you think your career does not entail public speaking. Well, this is where you're wrong because no matter what your job is, public speaking ultimately will come into the picture in some ways. This chapter, therefore, focuses on the significance of public speaking in our daily lives and on some specifics of the communication process.

Four General Types of Public Speakers
CATEGORYCHARACTERISTICS
The Avoider Does everything possible to avoid facing an audience. In some cases, avoiders seek careers that do not involve making presentations.

The Resister Becomes fearful when asked to speak. This fear may be strong. Resisters may not love to speak in public, but they have no choice. When they speak, they do so with great reluctance.

The Accepter Can do presentations but is not that enthusiastic to do them. Accepters occasionally give presentations and feel good about them. Occasionally the presentations can be quite persuasive, and satisfying.

The Seeker Always looks for opportunities to speak. Seekers understand that anxiety can be a stimulant that fuels enthusiasm during presentation. Seekers work hard at building their professional communication skills and self-confidence by speaking often.

What Roles Can Public Speaking Play in Your Life?

Success in public speaking can open a whole world of opportunities for you. It can help you conquer new frontiers. It can broaden your horizons through personal development, influence, and advances in your profession.

1. Public Speaking Improves Your Personal Development

In Abraham Maslow's hierarchy of needs, realizing man's self-worth ranks the highest. Giving speeches helps the speaker realize self-worth through the personal satisfaction he experiences whenever a good speech is given. The speaker becomes more confident especially when the audience responds positively. It also reduces anxiety when asked by an authority to speak in front of some people. There was once a student who dropped a course five times because he hated speaking in front of the class. But after a self-study on building up confidence, he decided to give public speaking a try and was successful. In fact, he came to enjoy the experience and even volunteered to give more speeches.

Through public speaking tools like research, conceptualization, and organization, you have a systematic and effective way of presenting your ideas; and thus, you will be able to express yourself better. You will also become more open to other people. Furthermore, speaking skills put you in a more significant role as you talk with people of high standing. Lastly, public speaking satisfies your sense of achievement when the audience accepts you warmly. This reflects your level of communication skills and acumen. All these contribute to your self-esteem.

2. Public Speaking Influences Your Society

It is not only you who can benefit from the art of communication but society as well. Most governments heed the voice of their citizens; with proper communication skills, you can represent the public in voicing out your rights and opinions.

An example of this would be a community discussion. Usually when a neighborhood holds regular meetings, it discusses certain issues or courses of action. In the discussion, various opinions are expressed and there you have a clear interplay of public speaking.

People from all walks of life need to speak in public, whether formally or otherwise. From kids reciting in school, to folks in a town meeting, to citizens voicing out national issues; from a plain market vendor, to a president of a company. There is really no way you can avoid public speaking.

3. Public Speaking Advances Your Profession

Public speaking can help in your career, and eventually, your finances. Usually, success is gauged by answers to questions like, "How long have you been in your job?" or "Do you hold an MBA degree or something similar?" However, researchers have proven that the best indicator of success in any profession is whether the person is often asked to give speeches. Those who give more speeches tend to have higher salaries than those who give less or no speeches.

Take this average engineer. She enrolls in a public speaking seminar that teaches two hours a week for six weeks. After two months, she is promoted to senior engineer! Her boss has been noticing her superb presentations.

The longer you work for an organization and the higher you climb the organizational ladder, the more your boss will ask you to preside over meetings and to give talks to the staff and subordinates or the clients. The higher your position, the more your responsibilities in leading people under you; and the more you must speak effectively. A manager once said, "From the chairman of the board to the assistant manager of the most obscure department, nearly everyone in business speaks in public or makes a speech at some time or the other."

Aside from big organizations like IBM and General Motors, small organizations and businesses in the country also need workers who are good public speakers. Take the high school coach, for example. If he is not persuasive enough to tell the school board that new gym equipment is needed, the school athletes might have to bear with the old gym equipment.

In the same way, if parents are not convincing enough when they complain about a school dress code, their children may end up still wearing uniforms in school. If salespeople cannot explain their products with a convincing sales pitch, then fewer people would buy their products. This is also true for nurses, doctors, firemen, police personnel and other professions. Even employees of General Motors meet regularly to make group decisions that they will present formally to management.

The bottom line is this: Whichever road you take, you will encounter instances that require you to speak in public.

Chpter 11: How To Overcome Your Fear Of Public Speaking

If you have a strong fear of public speaking, first of all take heart and know that you are not alone.In survey after survey, fear of public speaking ranks as one of the top fears that people have.In many of these studies, it is the number one fear that people have, even more so than death.The National Institute of Mental Health estimates that approximately 74% of people have some type of anxiety around public speaking.

The other important thing to keep in mind is that your fear of public speaking can be overcome.It isn't easy and does take some work and dedication, but it is definitely possible.

The first step towards overcoming your fear of public speaking is to really pinpoint what you are afraid of and examine these fears.So what exactly are you afraid of?Here are some of the most common things that people fear about getting up and speaking in front of a group of people:

Everyone staring at you

Afraid of making a mistake

Afraid of something embarrassing happening

Afraid of people laughing at you

Afraid that people will be bored and walk out

Afraid of offending someone

Let's take a closer look at some of these fears.

Everyone Staring At You

Yes it can be very stressful to stand in front of a group of people and feel that everyone is staring at you.However, think about this for a moment.When you are listening to someone speak, are you really paying that close of attention to every word and gesture that someone makes?If you really think about it, most of the time the answer is no.We are usually distracted by other thoughts and not really going over the speaker's performance with a fine tooth comb.

Afraid of Messing Up

Believe it or not, most people will not notice or know that you made a mistake.Only you know what you were planning to say.People are not looking for you to mess up, and most audiences will be rooting for you to give a good performance.If you do make a mistake, the best thing to do is just to move on and finish your speech.In many cases, people won't even realize you made a mistake, or if they do they will forget about it once your talk is over.

Afraid of Something Embarrassing Happening

We all have survived embarrassing moment in our lives, and making a speech is no different.The best thing you can do to avoid embarrassing moments from happening in the first place is adequate preparation and practice ahead of time.Similar to making a mistake, if something embarrassing happens, the best thing to do is to quickly handle the situation and move on.

Afraid of People Laughing at You

Most people in an audience can really emphasize with someone having to stand in front of a group of people and give a speech.Most people are going to have good will and want you to do well.The key here is to learn to connect with your audience so that you enjoy their presence rather than fearing them.

Afraid People Will Become Bored And Walk Out

It can be distracting for people to get up and leave during your speech.However, it is more likely they just need to use the restroom or are distracted by something else in their life that has nothing to do with your performance.Also remember the old adage, you can't please all the people all of the time.

Afraid of Offending Someone

Unless you are a very skilled and experienced public speaker, it is best to avoid controversial topics.Some people are easily offended, but the chances are if you stick with your presentation it is unlikely you will offend many people.

The key here is to really pinpoint what fears you have, and then really examine them.Once you really take a look at these common fears, you can see that most of our fears really don't have much validity.You are fearing that the worst will happen, and that everyone is against you.Obviously the chances of these things being true have very low odds.

Take the time to write down your specific fears and really examine what the most likely scenarios will be for your speech.Also remember that many of these situations can be avoided through being adequately prepared and connecting with your audience.In the next section, we'll go over some exercises you can do to change your mindset and approach the public speaking process with a more positive and relaxed attitude.

Chapter 12: The Open

Now to the break down. Baby steps to start.

The first of the three parts to any speech is the OPEN.

It's a lot like the headlines the nightly news cast gives at the start of the show - meaning this is what you will see tonight.

In other words, it's the first bit.

Doesn't sound too hard so far?

Stick with me here.

Let's set the scene - let's say you have been invited to give a talk at your old school. (Does this bring back any memories of grade school and show and tell or a class speech?)

Here are some examples of an 'EASY' open.

Hello my name is Neil.

Today I'd like to speak about an amazing trip I took with my family. We went to South Africa on safari in a wildlife game park.

Hello my name is Neil.

I was asked by the principal to share with you what happened when our softball team went off to the regional finals.

Hello my name is Neil

What I'm going to speak about today is a community project we are launching to help homeless people in our city.

Getting the picture here?

The same rules apply with the OPEN - no matter what level of audience you are speaking to.

The OPEN is simply giving your audience a clear idea of what you will be speaking about.

The OPEN **could** in fact be longer and more detailed, but we are starting at the absolute basics to make it easy to get going ... or at least **have a go at this.**

At this point, it is really important to be patient with yourself. You wouldn't shout at a baby when he or she is learning to walk would you?

Of course not, you would naturally give all the encouragement you can.

Do that for yourself as well. Be patient with yourself. Be kind to yourself. Encourage yourself.

Trust me, it will be worth it.

So are you with the program on what we do at the start of every speech?

It's the OPEN!

Please do not think I am being condescending here or trying to be smart. Remember, public speaking is the official number one fear in America and many other countries. We are trying to get past this fear.

Yes it's true - each of the three pieces may in fact expand further as you become more experienced, but it's the same basic formula.

It means that just about anyone can have a go at speaking, no matter what your background, education or current level of speaking ability.

Would you enter yourself in a marathon if you had just started jogging?Not likely.If you got the taste for running, you would naturally start out with light jogs and work up to something like a marathon over a period of time?

Same here with speaking. For people who are thinking about overcoming this fear of speaking in public and just starting out on this journey, where to start, and perhaps more importantly, **how to start** is the magic key that may unlock the door for you.

Now that we have an understanding of where to start and how to start, try a little exercise for yourself.

Imagine (OMG am I really going to try this?)

you have been invited to speak somewhere or have decided to try this out in front of your friends.

What would you talk about?

How would you OPEN?

Go with something easy- here's the set up.

You have been away on vacation and have just returned. There was no reception for your cell

phone where you were staying. No email, no internet connection.

Why would you go THERE? I can hear some of you thinking!

It's just you. Or you and your partner. You and a friend, family or whatever.

Your friends have gathered and they want to hear about your trip and it's the first time you have seen any of them since your return.(Your cell phone is still recharging)

You walk into a coffee shop where all your nearest and dearest have gathered and they know you are attempting to conquer your fear of public speaking.

What do you say?

Where do you start?

With an **OPENING** of course!

 "Hey everyone, thanks for coming."

(If you are with friends, they may start in on you here to make you feel 'more comfortable')

"We had an awesome time in the Amazon jungle but I am lucky to be standing here to be able to tell you about it."

Wow...good OPEN.

Your friends know you had an epic time.

They know you are going to share details about the trip.

They will be hanging on your every word to find out what happened to you.

This is the OPEN taken care of - you are out of the blocks and powering already.

Are you seeing how this OPEN works?

It becomes really simple when you understand how easy this is.

Go ahead and practice to yourself about how you would OPEN on other kinds of speeches.

Practice in the car while you are stuck in morning traffic. Practice while you are in the shower. Practice in the mirror while you are shaving, doing your hair or putting on make-up.

Start with the **OPEN**.

Once you get this simple formula DOWN, you will find yourself practicing an OPENING for all sorts of things.

Once you have tripped onto this formula fully, it will get easier and easier and eventually it will become second nature. You will become one of those people who could OPEN in their sleep!

Seriously, I hope you agree and will try it over and over. It only takes a couple of lines. Once you master it, you know TWO major things about speaking in public.

You know WHERE TO START

and HOW TO START.

Baby steps first.

"Hello my name **is (insert your own name here)** What I am going to talk about today is....... "

Keep trying it.Keep doing it over and over.You WILL get it down if you persist. Practice the OPEN for any subject you can think of.

Remember when you were learning to drive - especially a stick shift? Now it's second nature correct?

One final thought to get into your brain at this stage.

Be proud of yourself and your name.

Remember, if someone else can do it, YOU can too!

So go ahead and get the OPEN handled.

Knowing WHERE TO START and HOW TO START are two of the

biggest hurdles you will overcome.

You will go from that crushing fear to "I know what to do on at least two important bits."

Getting this first bit down is a genuine confidence builder.

Next is actually the **CLOSE**.

Why skip ahead to the end?

It's another easy bit that when you get that down, you will be 2 from 2.

How are you going so far?

If you got to this point, congratulations … you know how to OPEN and the next section is simply the other end ... the CLOSE. We will get to the BODY soon enough.

I encourage you to learn about the CLOSE as well as you have the OPEN.

Again, no matter what level of speaking you attain, this basic...the CLOSE is the same principle.

Chapter 13: Slaying The Beast: How To Deal With The Fright

Now that we know the causes of the fright, we have to deal with it. After all, it's not precisely the best of things to deliver a speech while shaking all the way from shoes to fingers, and there aren't a lot of topics that look very good if talked about while trembling nervously. (Those that **do** generally involve events of great trauma, and as such must be greatly dis-recommended.)

The first and most important thing to remember, and this extends to every profession and anything requiring public performance, is that it's perfectly all right to feel as nervous and afraid as all hell. This is natural, and this is expected, as that's the built-in fight-or-flight response kicking in.

The important thing is that, despite feeling it, the fright cannot be permitted to rule your response or your performance, and even more so, the fright **cannot and must not be shown.** Under no circumstances must a public speaker **look** afraid, even if he **is**.

Before anything, however, there's something that has to be said. Stage fright cannot be entirely eliminated, only reduced. The fight-or-flight response is built too far down to get at with such crude tools as we have available, and thus any speaker – indeed, any performer – will have to deal with the fright every time he's nearby the stage and waiting to go on.

Whether novice, seasoned, or hardened veteran, whether musician, actor, speaker, or professional strawman, whether a newcomer or a star or Elvis Presley himself, all of these have felt the fright and have had to deal with it.

(Yes, Elvis. He in fact confessed that he'd always had the fright before a show and never gotten over it. Consider it a point of comfort; if Elvis of all people dealt with stage fright and still rocked out in front of an audience, then you can, too.)

Now that that's done with, let's take you through a few sections on how to go about kicking the fright in the teeth.

Ready Aye Ready: Preparation

As with all things, it never hurts to be prepared. Unless you're a specialist in coming up with a speech on the fly – and those exist, though it's something of an acquired skill – it's best to come at a speech after having previously rehearsed it.

Snag a friend, or family member, or anyone willing to listen, into a place large enough to accommodate all of them, and deliver. Their feedback is going to be useful, and some of them may well have something useful for you, or have spoken publicly in the past – you never know, after all.

Don't overdo it, however. There can be such a thing as over-preparedness, and it's easy to feel when it comes to public speaking. Rehearse as much as you need, but mind that you don't get tired of your material.

This is another area where memorised speeches fail, because they're not quite easy to alter on the fly after you get feedback. Come at a speech from several directions before the day, so you can see how best to go at it when the time comes.

If at all possible, try and get a look around the place you'll be speaking before the appointed time, and better still, see if you can't rehearse there. Check everything, familiarise yourself with the location, and get to know the room or stage, or whatever it is you'll be speaking in.

This'll take some concerns off your mind, and moreover, a feel for the room is nearly as important as a feel for the audience. If you don't know your ground, you're likely to be dropped into a sinkhole.

Again, if it's possible, try and find out a few details about your audience. Age, socio-economic background, probable interests, and other such. Any of these could provide some means at grabbing your audience's attention, as an apathetic audience is no audience at all. Hook them in, and you've got them made.

Many are going to overlook this detail, focusing on their speech and the stuff surrounding it, but spare some time for your clothing. Don't go in with stuff you just bought and aren't used to yet, not unless there's no other alternative. If you aren't used to a new outfit and don't know how you can move in it, leave it at home, and better instead to get an outfit you know and have broken in.

If you know you look good in your outfit, and it makes you feel good, then go with that. The same goes for shoes; take a comfortable pair that you've walked in, and forget the new pair you haven't broken in yet.

If you don't think yourself ready for the big stage yet, then there are always classes or seminars for public speaking. (Yes, they exist.) Ask around your local schools and universities and see if you can't attend a few; if nothing else, you'll have the company of those in the same boat, needing to deliver a speech yet not knowing how to go about things.

Alternatively, there are professional coaches for public speaking or perhaps Toastmasters clubs; a bit of digging and asking around can generally get results.

Whatever you choose, just remember: One speech will generally not be enough to decide your career, not this early, not unless you're highly (un)lucky. Mastery takes time and work, and though there are naturals at things, even they need to hone their skills to really get going.

Studying the great orators might also yield some valuable lessons — after all, one learns from the masters. However, be mindful that you don't copy their style, not unless you're quite sure you won't get caught. Public speaking demands a certain something straight from the heart, and there's no future in copying someone else.

Instead, use your model, or models, as inspiration, and shape your own style. It's always better to be yourself, instead of being someone else. You're not that person, after all — you're **you.**

Five Minutes To Go

It's nearly enough a truism that the wait for something is more nerve-wracking than the thing itself. This remains true for public speaking, and it's in that time between arrival at the venue and delivering your speech that the fright is going to hit hardest. Stress will be at a high, and your nerves will be up and sparking.

Best, then, to reduce the amount of stress and nervousness you'll be getting when you arrive. While you rehearse, see if you can't get someone with a camera to record – audio or video – your performance.

Then play the record while you're on the way or waiting (but make sure nobody sees you, if the audience is already there) so you can review your performance and see where you can improve things.

Besides, once you see or hear yourself on tape or video, then you can assure yourself: "I've done this before, and I can do it again."

The only difference being that there's an audience the second time around. Odd, how that affects so many people so negatively so as to bring about the fright.

So you're there and waiting, with the fright tapping your shoulder. Since it isn't a concrete thing we can punch in the face, we instead go about defeating the fright in different manners. Any relaxation techniques you can think of will come in handy, and the more inconspicuous, the better.

Breathing exercises are the best, as it'll take a very perceptive audience member to notice anything. Tense and release muscles without moving the body part in question; that'll get some flex in without a lot of jerking about, and it'll help in controlling the shakes.

Try a familiar scent, too, something you associate with calmness or confidence. Your significant other's favourite scent, for instance, sprayed onto a handkerchief or a Kleenex and smelled discreetly.

Or a scent that's known to relax the body — jasmine, chamomile, or pine, with a similar deployment. There are a lot of people who don't put much stock in aromatherapy, but the rule is, as always, whatever works.

No matter what you try, no matter how you go about preparing yourself in those very stressful minutes before you have to go up and speak, there's something you ought to keep in mind. It's an interesting, and possibly the most important detail, about the fright:

Most of it comes around **before** one gets on the stage. By the time you step on up, it's already fading away, and when you're really hitting your stride, there's a lot of other things to worry about than your own fear.

Chapter 14: Opening Of The Speech: Start With A Spark

The opening of the speech is very critical for the success of your speech. In the era of ever-shrinking attention span and instant distraction devices like cell phone, it is very important for the speaker to organize his introduction very thoughtfully. It is said the audience often judge a speaker within 30 seconds of his beginning. If one fails to create an impression and hook the audience, it is very difficult to win over the audience.

Start with a spark:

The way you begin your speech determine the tone of your speech. "Well began is half done" is very true when it comes to public speaking. In the wake of mass communication like Television and 24x7 internet, which has made easy access to world-class speeches of leaders and politicians across the world. Moreover, TED talks is full of good speeches. These accessibility has made the expectation of audience much higher. Any boring start would put off the audience. Generally, it takes three times effort to win back their attention. It is not an easy task, given the very low attention span and a plethora of distractions. Dazzle the audience with a striking start and get to the point as quickly as possible. Your start should be creating a suitable platform for your speech to take off. However, trying to get attention for the attention sake would boomerang and make you look shallow and ordinary speaker.

Starting with humor or joke, in the beginning is not an ideal way to start unless you are doing a stand-up comedy or giving a humorous speech. It would make the audience take you lightly. It may project you as a casual person who would waste their time with trivia. If you are a confident speaker and good at humor, you can start with humor but keep it very short and then jump on to the topic. However, in corporate and business set up, try to avoid it because if it goes wrong it would be a blunder.

How to open your speech

(1) The Mystic pause: The attention of the audience is at the peak just before a speaker speaks. A deliberate and confident silence before you start speaking is a very powerful way of arousing curiosity among the audience and creates subtle impact. It adds to your presence on the stage. This display an air of confidence. It gives you time to smile and make eye contact thereby connect with the audience even without uttering a single word. When you pause before speaking it makes the audience to draw into you. It makes them feel and expect that something interesting is about to come.

(2) Tell a story: It is one of the most effective way of starting your speech. You can start with a relevant story to your topic. For instance, if your topic is courage, you can share a personal story. Here's my personal story on courage:

The water in the swimming pool had always mirrored back one question: How long would you procrastinate? Before the pool could say, have courage, dear! I usually walked off. I took the cue but never took the real action. However, as I was reaching my late 20s, I thought and asked myself, if not now when? It was December 2010, when I decided to learn swimming. My senior colleague helped in learning but there was no progress even after 10 days. It was Saturday morning and he had left for Chennai to meet his family. I was feeling bad that he is not around. However, I took the risk and went alone in the pool. I tried swimming for some time. After 30 minutes of trying in vain suddenly I could swim. Yes, on my own I could swim. I realized that my courage to go solo on that morning made me learn swimming.

If your topic is fear, you can use the following story to start

There was a dog who lost his way and entered in a glass room of a palace, which had thousands of small mirror on the wall and roof. The dog saw his own image and took it as other dogs. He barks at them out of fear and the reflections bark back. He again barked at his own image and then after few hours died out of exhaustion and fear. Such is the condition of human being. Fear is nothing but a false notion of reality. As a person who attempts to speak on the stage, we too fear from our own self-created perception. We see hundreds of eyes looking at us and what they might be thinking about us. Oh! they must be laughing or making a mockery of me. It is all self-created perception.

You can use appropriate stories to substantiate your message. However, sharing your personal story is best. It has the greatest power of convincing your audience about the topic. Because most of the time audience wants to know how your life was altered or affected or how you have fought back or adopted the learning from the topic.

(3) Share interpersonal experience: Besides the personal story, you can also share interpersonal experience, which has relevance to the topic. For instance, Indian Prime Minister Narendra Modi's in his Sept. 28 speech in New York City's Madison Square Garden began his speech by sharing his experience. He said,

"A few years ago I was in Taiwan. Back then I wasn't a chief minister and I had an interpreter with me. After a few days, we got acquainted and he asked me one day, "If you don't mind, may I ask you a question?" I said, "Yes, I won't mind, please go ahead." He asked again, "Are you sure you won't mind?" I said, "No, I won't. Please go ahead." He was still hesitant. And then he said, "I've heard that India is a land of black magic, snakes and snake charmers, that people play around with snakes; Is this all true?' I replied, "No, not anymore. Our nation has developed a lot since then. Our ancestors used to play with the snake, but today we play with the mouse." And our youth today move the world with their mouse!"

This was an excellent way to highlight the progress of new India. It demonstrated the power of Indian youth taking the country to another level. It was witty with a powerful message. It is important to choose such personal experience so that audience could also easily relate to themselves.

(4) A striking question: Asking question is another effective way of starting a speech with a bang. However, often the novice use it to their utter failure and surprise. They overlook the fact that if they don't create the right impression and create rapport with the audience, chances of getting a response is very bleak. The speaker needs to be confident and create connection with the audience to get the positive response from them.

The questions should be universal and such that most of the audience would concur with it. Here few sample question: How many of you think that you can do better with existing resources and time?

How many of you believe that your talent surpasses your current job or income?

How many of you wants to live a vibrant life?

How many of you consider health very important?

(5) Startling statistics and facts: Starting with quoting startling fact related to the topic is a very good way to get audience attention. Such statistics or facts should be striking and not very common. Further, you should not go on explaining the statement in details. Its utility is to kindle curiosity and trigger thoughts and feeling towards the topic. "The main part of intellectual education is not the acquisition of facts but learning how to make facts live." (Oliver Wendell Holmes, American Judge) For instance,

- Road accident in India kills 2100 people every week which is four times of security forces killed in a year due to terrorism.
- 500 miliion tonne (40% of the total food grains) in Indian godowns gets wasted due to pest and climatic conditions. This amount is enough to feed half of our population for one year.
- 70% of Indians are obese. 80% of Women in India are anemic.

(6) Use a prop A symbolic physical object or action: A picture is worth a thousand words. When you use a prop, which could be a pen, tie, an envelope or letter, Identity card, currency note depending on the topic of your speech.

What it does is to capture attention immediately. It creates curiosity and enables you to introduce your theme or idea in a very effective manner.

(7) Poem: Using few lines of the famous poem which is in direct relevance to your topic is also a good way to begin a speech. The poem has the effect of easing the audience and provides an apt background. However, the poem should not be long and if it is long only a few relevant lines should be quoted.

(8) Using statement in foreign/another language: Have you observed, politicians and celebrity when they visit abroad and address the audience by using one or two sentences of the local language. Invariably, they get immediate applause and hooting from the audience. Use of foreign language is an out of box way of starting your speech. Conversely, you can use Sanskrit or any other language in the beginning of your speech and then explain the meaning. It will grab the attention of the audience.

(9) Avoid long introduction: Public speakers both the novice and the experienced one often end up giving a very long introduction. Not coming to the point quickly can ruin you speech by distracting your audience. Howsoever good your introduction may appear to be, don't keep it very long. Introduce the topic or come to the central message and harp on it. As a speaker, your focus should be on the one key message that you want to convey.

(10) Connect with the present event: One of the best ways to invite the attention of the audience is to start with something which is in news and link it to your topic. Whatever may be your topic you can find something happening that field. Therefore, while writing your speech do some research and find out what is the news item or recent happening that is relevant to your topic. It will immediately enable everyone in the audience to find a common ground.

(11) Tell the audience what is there for them: An introduction should be a preview for what lies ahead. However, the audience is more interested in knowing why they should listen to you, what benefit or lessons or knowledge they would get at the end of the speech. It is important to tell or indicate what is there in store for them.

Blunders in opening of speech

There are some common blunders that speakers do in the beginning of their speech:

(a) To introduce themselves even after being already introduced.

(b) Being casual by asking redundant questions like: How you are doing? What about the nice weather? Did you face any problem reaching the venue? Did you have good breakfast?

(c) Being too common:

- Let me begin with an interesting story of my childhood.
- Let me ask you something very interesting.
- I would start with a very humorous joke.
- Let me tell you what I am going to speak about in my speech (and you give out all the content in brief and there is nothing for audience to explore and anticipate)
- Do you know what I am going to tell you

today?

- Can you guess what I am talking about or what I will be speaking today? Any guesses? Guys!

A speaker should always remember that stage time is given to him so that he can deliver something valuable in the form of information, entertainment, inspiration etc. Remember the story: In Japan, once a leader came 10 minutes late and the organizer was very disappointed and he conveyed the same to the leader. However, the leader said, I am just 10 minutes late. The organizer then said, Sir by coming 10 minutes late, you have wasted the 10 minutes of 50,000 people that means 0.5 million minutes of this country and it is a colossal waste.

(d) Starting with humor: Use of humor in the introduction is fraught with risk for these reasons. (i) Humor is not easy. Until one is very confident, it is risky to attempt. (ii) Failed humor fails your speech (iii) Humor present you as casual and nonserious speaker (iv) Humor may not be needed in most of the speeches, even if it is needed try it after introduction part of the speech.

A speaker must have the respectful attitude towards the time and attention of the audience. It enables you to give your best in public speaking. Make the audience know and feel that you are worthy of their time and attention.

The attention is on the peak in the beginning. Therefore, the speaker should use this opportunity to get audience attention and begin with a good start for his speech. There is no best way to begin your speech, it all depends on your comfort level, personality, audience and occasion of the speech. However, it is ideal to experiment with the different way of introduction rather than sticking to one style.

Chapter 15: The Why

This has to do with the purpose of your speech. Do you want to increase your audience's awareness in a certain area or do you want to encourage them to change their attitudes, or behaviors, or both-- about something? Having your purpose clear is essential as this will dictate the content of your speech and the ways you present it.

Increasing your audience's understanding or awareness….

Suppose from your own research you find that not many Americans know about the game of cricket and you'd like to give a speech about the game. Or maybe someone asks you to speak about it knowing that you are originally from a country that not only plays the game but is crazy about it.

The purpose of your speech would depend on what you want from the audience. Do you want them to know that such a game exists for those of them who don't know about it? Perhaps some members do know about it, but the knowledge is quite superficial and you'd like to deepen it. Then your general goal or purpose is to **inform** them about the game.

Or, suppose you are aware that your audience already knows about the game but they believe it is boring and takes days to end. You might want to provide them with more detailed information about the game in an effort to change their attitude towards it and actually try to encourage them to actually watch a few televised matches or even try their hand at the game by checking out a local sports club that plays it. Here, you are evidently trying to persuade your audience that by the end of your speech, they will have a change in attitude regarding this game that you **love** and are **passionate** about. Of course, I'll expect your love or passion for this game to come out in the delivery of your speech and that these emotions would strike a chord in your audience—especially sports lovers.

Chapter 16: Understanding Communication Methods

Communication is the method by which we pass information between individuals and organisations. There are a large number of communication methods available to us. Unfortunately, the wide variety of methods means that many people now are reaching information overload, and it is becoming more and more difficult to separate important and effective information from the
'noise' of other communications going on around them.

It is for this reason that it is becoming more and more important to employ highly effective communication techniques to ensure that your messages and information are delivered effectively. Unfortunately, it is very simple to slip into the trap of ineffective communication. There are many examples where a lack of preparation undermines the delivery of the message or misses the needs of the audience, which means that the communication is ignored entirely.

Effective communication needs to be:

- relevant and meet the needs of the audience
- authoritative, believable and trusted
- delivered in a way which presents the organisation or the individual in a professional manner.

This ebook will give you a series of tools and techniques which will allow you to ensure that any communication you use meets these requirements and gains the best impact with the audience.

The fact that an organisation has always given a presentation to illustrate new products, for example, does not negate the fact that you could consider a facilitated workshop or meeting. It is important for each and every

communication you wish to deliver to consider:
- What do we need to communicate?
- What is our audience?
- What would the best way to communicate this be?

If you consider these simple questions and get the right answers you will ensure that you are delivering the information in the most relevant way.

The Confident Presenter
- Introduction to presentations and events
o What is the reason for events
o What is the general audience expectation
- Overcoming fear or stage-fright
o Ensuring that you always have the confidence to deliver at your best
- Having the confidence to present
o Techniques to reduce pre-presentation nerves
- Breathing Exercises

- o Concentrating on breathing and not your nerves
- Mind changers
- Smile and your brain smiles with you!
- o Using music to drive your mood
- Preparing to succeed (Positive thinking in practice)
- o Dealing with doubt
- o Transferring belief
- Becoming an 'Alpha Presenter'
- o Understanding pack mentality with presentations
- Section Review

Introduction to presentations and events

What comes into your mind when you think of a presentation? Is it excitement, anticipation and interest?

Unfortunately, the answer is very likely to be none of the above. Over time many of us have become subjected to poorly created presentations: pages of bullet points on the projector screen; a speaker who didn't hold our interest; need I go on? Technology such as PowerPoint has allowed us to create excellent presentations; however, it also allows us to create the complete opposite.

We need to understand that presentations are more than electronic files: we actually need to understand a bit about the psychology of presentations and learn some secrets which are more common in film and theatre.

Before we look at the presentation tools, we need to look at the presenter. There are two major failings which are identified by people when they see a 'poor' presentation: the presenter and the presentation. We will start with the presenter and how you can become confident, believable and a truly powerful presenter!

Overcoming fear or stage-fright

Does public speaking make you nervous? This is a serious question which you may think has two answers:

- Yes – I am not happy giving presentations in public.

- No – I am a confident presenter.

There is of course a third response, which is that you have some nerves before a presentation but you do not let them hold you back. The nervousness you feel comes from the fact that you are stepping up in front of an audience (often of your peers) and therefore you will need to put your head above the parapet. You may perceive that there is a high risk of failure ('what if they don't like me?') and you may not feel confident that you know what to say.

I would be lying if I could tell you how to completely conquer stage fright. In fact we really don't want to get rid of our stage fright or presentation fear. This is because to do so runs the risk of making your presentation dry or over-rehearsed. In fact if you talk to famous actors they will often tell you that that still have some controlled nerves there before they go on stage, despite the fact that this is their 'day job' and they are very experienced.

It is controlled nerves which will give you an edge and allow you to give amazing presentations. I have given many thousands of presentations to large and small audiences around the world and I can assure you that the day I do not feel that
tingle of nervous excitement before I speak is the day I will give up, because I know that is the day I will not be ready to shine on stage.

This ebook will give you tools and techniques which will allow you to manage any pre-show nerves, and also prepare for anything that may happen during a presentation.

Having the confidence to present

There are a number of techniques to build and support your confidence. The most important one is to ensure that you are fully prepared for your presentation, ensuring that you have confidence in your subject and what you are going to say (we will cover this later in this ebook). Once

you are confident in your subject you are a long way towards giving a confident presentation. To help you further you can use two additional techniques:
- breathing exercises
- mind changers

Breathing Exercises

It is important to remember the following:
- your breathing will affect your voice and projection - learning to control your breathing will allow you to improve the projection and clarity of your voice.
- your breathing can be affected by nerves.
- you can also control your nerves by controlling your breathing.

You have to consider; how often do you think about breathing? It is an automatic function which we never have to think about; it just happens.

Try the following simple breathing exercise:
- take a deep breath in through your mouth

- breath out SLOWLY through your nose (mentally count the seconds that it takes you to breath out)
- concentrate on your breathing and repeat this at least five more times.

There are two benefits, firstly you will get more oxygen into your lungs and therefore feed your brain, and secondly the act of concentration allows you to think about something other than your nerves. Distraction is a good technique; we use it with children and it still works with us as adults. Force yourself to take a moment and think of something else. This is a simple technique that can be carried out anywhere and at any time.

Mind changers

The second simple technique is the use of mind changers. These are two simple tricks which you can use to up your energy and make you feel better. They may sound very simplistic, however, I can promise you that they are very powerful and can work a treat!

First of all, smile. Even if you are feeling like you really don't want to (in fact, particularly if you feel like you don't want to). Then use a mantra: tell yourself out loud that you are great and that you can succeed in your presentation. Repeat it a few times, be confident and really speak out.

There are two techniques at work here. The acts of smiling (and other emotions) are handled by a lower, more primitive part of our brains. If you physically smile the lower brain tells the upper brain that you are happy. It can help you improve the way you feel. If you support this with the second technique, a strong vocal message, it becomes a very powerful, mood changing tool.

Another thing to use is music. We will see later how we can change an audience mode with music, and it can work for you as a presenter also. Think of your favourite upbeat track, how does it make you feel when you hear it on the radio?

Think of a track that you would sing along to in the car or shower (or tap the steering wheel if you are not the singing sort!) Pick a track that appeals to you and makes you feel happy (I use 'Can you feel it?'
by the Jackson Five, however you no doubt have better musical taste!). Good music is great for changing your mood. Look at a good movie; they will use slow mournful music when the action is sad or downbeat. (How does this make you feel?) In the same way, happy upbeat music can make you feel great.

Make sure you are musically charged before you go to your presentation by playing your 'mantra track' before you get ready for your presentation..

Preparing to succeed

Before you start any presentation you need to ask yourself if you have any doubts about it. This is important because if you cannot convince yourself, you will not persuade your audience. Before you start speaking you must believe in what you are going to say...

This is the transfer of belief. An audience can detect (from your vocal tone and body language) when you do not believe in what you are talking about. This can seriously affect the acceptance of your presentation.

You need to eliminate any doubts you may have about your presentation, so you need to be sure of the content and subject area. Think about the old saying

'Believe you will fail and you will.' This is true for presentations, but can also be paraphrased as 'Doubt your content and your audience will also doubt it.'

Becoming an 'Alpha Presenter'

In the animal kingdom, pack animals (such as dogs) have a leader called the Alpha animal; this is the animal who leads all of the other animals in the pack.

The same should be true in presentations. You as the presenter should be the leader when you are speaking and be seen to be the leading individual. In this way you have control of the audience and also their respect. You should ask yourself, do you have an alpha role when you are presenting? Do you allow the audience to take control of your presentation or do you have full control? When you consider your presentations you should remember that you should:

- have control of the room – this means that if you are speaking you should look to ensure you are the only one speaking. If audience members are talking, pause and see if they stop. (If not, see the techniques for dealing with difficult people later in the course)
- be in control of your content – you demonstrate that you clearly have belief in your subject
- be in control of your confidence – you should 'own the stage', this means that you do not seem timid or apprehensive about your presentation. (The audience can smell fear!)

If you think of yourself as an Alpha Presenter you will be able to bring together the management of pre-event nerves and belief in a whole attitude.

Section Review

You have undertaken the first step of becoming a perfect presenter, so to recap:

- the presenter is key to the presentation
- whereas we cannot completely remove stage-fright we can control it and use it to our advantage
- thinking about your breathing can reduce your nerves and give you time to think and be calm
- be ready to change your mind by smiling and positive vocal phrases
- use upbeat music to move your mind to a more positive state
- get rid of doubts; have confidence in yourself and your presentation
- be in control – you are the Alpha Presenter Now, let's move on and look at the presentation itself.

Chapter 17: Presentation

You may have heard this before. This is where practice, practice, practice, comes in. Record yourself on CD and video if you can. I will be happy to review it for you.

Delivery is the first thing you need consider. My best advice, be yourself, let it come naturally. If you are speaking too fast, you probably nervous. With practice, you will gain confidence.Your appearance should be professional, over dress for the occasion. ENJOY YOURSELF AND SMILE!

Eye contact should be natural and look around the room at each person, only for a few seconds. Your gestures can be planned, but try being as natural as possible. Your body will speak louder than words. Find your own style.

Use your voice, play with it, have fun with it-- your pitch, rate. If you want to get your Audience's attention, whisper. A pause or silence can be very effective as well.Be Yourself. Have Fun!

Visual Aids - What is nice about visual aids is you can use them as your guide/outline. It keeps you on track, so you don't need notes.

NOTE: Visual Aids should be simple and easy to read, the less information the better. Make the writing big enough so those in the back can see and read your visual aids.

Visual aids can really enhance your presentation, but remember it is you they came to see. Use them wisely, and make them concentrate on you. Use them, then get rid of them.

Laptop Computer with wall/screens: Make sure you set it up and preview your presentation.

Hand-Outs - do not give them out ahead of time, if possible. Use them as you go. They will be and reading ahead. Again, you want them to concentrate on you. Be sure your handouts are well designed out and are an asset to your presentation.

Charts - Make sure everyone can see what you have. And don't clutter them with too much information.

Flip Charts - Have these ready before the presentation. Key _ Work backwards. When preparing flip charts use every other page and start with your first graphic in the middle of the flip chart sheets, skip a sheet, do the next, skip a sheet, do the next. When you are ready to start, open it to your first graphic and cover it with a sheet when you are done. As you continue with your presentation, when you done talking about this graphic, flip the next sheet forward covering the graphic. Keep doing this. Remember, keep your audience watching you. It is easier to work this way.

Chalk/White Boards - Great! But be careful with them. Don't turn your back to your audience or talk to the board. Write on it, demonstrate/describe, turn around, talk about what is there, then erase it.

Microphones - lapel, portable, omni, stand alone. Be sure it is working, test it. Practice with it. Talk across the microphone. Try to keep most of your face showing to the audience.

Podiums/Lecterns - Here is a big mistake even professionals make. You speak on the podium and behind the lectern. A podium is a riser, a raised platform. The lectern maybe free standing or sitting on a table.

Always get to your speaking engagement early, so you can check everything out, make sure everything is working properly.'

Environment

I'm talking about the comfort of your audience here. Keep the room well ventilated - 68 – 70 degrees. Make sure there is enough room and everyone can see you. Check out the sound system, lighting, shades, windows.

After lunch, you will need to keep them awake.

Room Arrangement

The layout of the room is important to your success and your audience's comfort.

>>U-shaped Table

This is best when you want participation and expect a lot of discussion. It is good for face to face communication. Ideal for groups up to 20.

>>Classroom

Good for a large group and long sessions. Suitable for work/lecture, instructional or training meetings. Angled position lets participants see one another.

>>Center Table

Good for small rooms and small group (no more than 12).

>>Auditorium or Theater

For large groups when you expect little or no participation. Your major concern is that everyone can see your screen and visible to everyone.

>>Amphitheater

The best setting for short or moderately long speeches with no participation. Permits seating of more people and gives a good view of the speaker and screen. No recommended for long presentations.

Projector Arrangement

Office Meeting Room

In a small office, you can use a projector on a desktop. The speaker stands behind the desk with the screen or wall behind them.

Dual Overhead Projectors

2 projectors can be used in most room arrangements. The major advantage is that is allows the

speaker to introduce a series of key points on one screen while using the second to show more details.

Projector Arrangement

The speaker and projector are placed in a standard position. The screen should be in a corner at an angle, so the speaker won't obstruct the view for some participants. It should be at a 40-degree angle or less. A white matte screen with keystone eliminator is a good choice.

Viewing Distances

Visuals need to be seen. Either the projected image is too small or the audience is too far from the screen. If they can't see, there is too much information on the slides or transparencies.

Slides: If the slides design can be read from 8 times its height, it should be legible when projected.

BONUSES

Bonus #1 - Fun Voice Exercises

We take our voices for granted. A lot of tension forms in our throats and larynx. These simple fun exercises can help you.

6 Steps to a Better Voice

1. Feel your throat muscles and jaw when you are speaking. Note the tenseness

2. Open mouth wide. Yawn and say _Ho Hum. _ Close your lips. As you do, drop your jaw and waggle it from side to side.

3. Repeat the yawning and humming. Note how the throat muscles loosen & Removes strain.

4. Open mouth wide, drop your jaw, exaggerate your lip and jaw movements. Say the following words slowly: Prolong the sounds. Annunciate carefully. HANG, HARM, LANE, MAIN, LONE, LOOM.

5. Lightly massage your throat muscles with your fingers to check for tightness.

6. Drop your jaw and relax the throat. Prolong the sounds. Open wide and use a monotone voice. Say: NAH, HAY, NEE, NO, NOO.

Try this several times a day. You should see an improvement. in your speaking voice.

Tummy Bounce

Take a breath through the mouth for three seconds, and immediately let it out as you say 10 "Ha's" in succession, using one breath. Keep the back of your throat open.

Ka-Ga-Ha

Open mouth wide and open back of your throat.

Say _ka-ka-ka-ka-ka-_ As many times as you can with one breath.

Again Say; _Ga-ga-ga-ga-ga-ga_ - As many times as you can with one breath.

Again With; _ha-ha-ha-ha-ha-ha_ - As many times as you can with one breath.

Now With _ka-ga-ha _, _ka-ga-ha _, _ka-ga-ha _, _ka-ga-ha _ - As many times as you can with one breath.

The Lion

1-Open eyes wide

2-Open Mouth wide

3-Extend tongue and hold for 8 seconds.

This exercise improves circulation, washes away germs, prevents wrinkles and sore throats, drains stress. Try it. See how it feels.

Vitalic Breath

1-Inhale a few short quick breaths through the nose

2-Open mouth, expel quickly with one blast.

2 or 3 times only, or you will get dizzy.

#2 Bonus - Meeting Planning Checklist
Meeting Objective:

___
Date _____ Time _____ to _____.

Place _____

___Room Reserved

___Agenda Meeting Notice (___prepared, ___sent)
___Visuals Prepared
Participants
Meeting Materials
___ Note pads, pencils ___Name/place cards ___ Name Badges
___ Hand-outs

_____

Equipment
___Laptop Computer
___Marking Pens
___Microphone
___Lectern
___Extension Cord

___ _____

Refreshments
___ Coffee ___Juice ___ Soft Drink
___ Lunch

Post Meeting
___Action Minutes
___Next Meeting

#3 Bonus – "How to Win Over Your Fears"

If you really want to do something you will always find a way. But if you don't want to do it, you will find excuses.

The easiest way to combat fear is by not using excuses. Instead, you need to look for positive approaches to accomplish your goal. If you want to start a business, attend a meeting at the Better Business Bureau. Read some national magazines like "Income Opportunities" or "Spare Time."

Start reading the business section of your newspaper. Gather some ideas and do a little reading before jumping into a business. Surely you can find some spare time to read.

Also, begin associating yourself with people who are in their own business already. If you're afraid to go out and make new friends, attend local business-related seminars in your community.

Start watching television shows that are related to business. You'll eventually find people to associate with who know others and you'll be the part of a new crowd - the motivating ones!

FEAR is always your enemy. Look at it this way: If you never try, FEAR wins by 100%.

However, if you do try, FEAR only has a chance of winning by 50%. If you needed a place to live and only had $10 to your name would you allow FEAR to win and make you homeless? No, most of us would find a job or borrow the money to have a roof over our heads! FEAR is the root of failure, depression and lifelong problems. Are you going to let FEAR ruin your life?

FEAR also will cause you to lose out on many other things in life. If you FEAR the boss at work is going to fire you _ it will naturally be on your mind day in and day out. It will eventually wear you down and you will begin making mistakes on the job. You will also get depressed and build up resentments that may have never been there in the first place.

Facing FEAR head on is the best way to combat it. If you think the boss is going to fire you, go up and ask him. It takes guts, but isn't it better than putting yourself through many months of agonizing torture?

Are you full of so much FEAR to even ask him because you think it will trigger him to say "yes" when he might not have been considering it at all? Believe me, asking a boss "if" they are thinking about firing you will put you in no different position than you are now. In fact, it will have the opposite effect. The boss will more than likely respect you for your candidness and ability to face FEAR head-on.

Is FEAR holding you back from a lot of things? Are you afraid to confront people and tell them how you really feel? Do you smile in their face, talk about them behind their back? What's so hard about being truthful but using tact? Doesn't it get rid of FEAR and solve many problems?

Complaining is also an act that emotionally drains you and goes together with FEAR. In fact, FEAR is normally the root of any complaint.

People don't want to admit their FEAR so they will complain to release some tension. This is a crazy merry-go-round! Instead of complaining, try to find ways to solve the problem.

4.Bonus Analyze Your Audience ---- The Face Reading Way!

I sometimes have trouble with public speaking.Seeing so many faces in the audience can blow my mind. I can see each person's personality. If I let it, it can disrupt my presentation.But I've learned to live with it.

Now I'd like to share with you, some tips you can use with your audience.Or if you're a teacher, you can use this on your students.

A person is more open and positive when the lower lid of the eye is more curved. When the lower lid straightens out and becomes flat, they have become guarded or defensive.

2. A hook nose is good with money and business.(Stick to business with this person and ask for financial help.)

3. A turned up nose likes to be of service. (Ask them for help, directions, assistance)

4. A large mouth is talkative and generous. (Use small talk, and about their family.They like to be around people.)

5. A small mouth is brief and tight. (Come to the point quickly and don't keep them waiting.)

6. Eyes that are close together are impatient. (Be on time.Trust them to get things done right.)

7. Eyes that are far apart are tolerant.(Expect tardiness & easy-going behavior. Set deadlines & give reminders)

8. Eyebrows that are high are selective and formal. (Mind your manners. Be on your best behavior. Use courtesies.)

9. Eyebrows that are set low are informal and easy going. (Warn them about

protocol.Let them sell.Ask them to host a party.)

Each face reveals its personality, destiny, strengths, and weaknesses.What a person thinks about most of the time shows up on their face. So, their face becomes a road map of their mind.

Chapter 18: Tips Before Engaging In Public Speaking

Do you need to deliver a speech in a day or two? Are you now nervous and conscious of what might happen on the day when you deliver your speech? Before you jump into conclusions, it is important to remind yourself of the things that you need to do before you engage in public speaking. This chapter will share to you some tips so that you will feel less nervous and less afraid before you speak in public.

Even if you are just a few minutes away from delivering your speech, it is important to practice your speech thoroughly. Look for a mirror, and try delivering your speech to yourself. If you are not comfortable seeing yourself, then you can try delivering your speech while facing the wall. Deliver your speech repetitively, keeping in mind the parts in which you commit mistakes. Do them over again, while avoiding committing the same mistakes until you get it perfectly. Once you do, rest for a while and then do it again. This is important because you do not only need to know what your speech is; rather you need to be able to master it. Unless you are comfortable that you can deliver it perfectly during your actual presentation, do not stop. As the saying goes, practice makes perfect.

It is also important if you try to condition yourself even before you begin your speech. Be prepared to receive criticisms. You may not be able to please everyone, but that's completely fine. It does not mean, however, that you will think of negative things. You only need to prepare yourself so that you will not be surprised when some of the audience get bored and became less interested with your speech.

If you still have enough time, it will also be helpful if you keep recording your practice speeches. Doing so will help you evaluate how you sound, what your grounds for improvement are, what goes well, and what does not. Improve on the parts where you think you need improvement. Do it again and again until you finally get it right.

It will help you a lot if you practice in front of a mentor or someone who knows how to speak properly in front of people. By doing so, you will know what and how to improve. Constructive criticisms are necessary for you to become an effective public speaker.

Now that you know what you have to do before delivering your speech, the next important thing to know is what to do when you are already delivering your speech. Fear does not subside immediately after you begin your speech. You may even experience them the whole time that you are speaking. What do you do during these circumstances? These things will be discussed in the chapter to follow.

Chapter 19: The First Honey

There is always a first honey to everything in life.

Before Christ was revealed to the public John the Baptist had gone ahead to prepared the way for Him. For Christ, John the Baptist was the **first honey** that attracted and pointed people to the Savior.

The Bible referred to John the Baptist as the voice of him crying in the wilderness. "Then said they unto him, Who art thou? That we may give an answer to them that sent us. What sayest thou of thyself? He said, I am the voice of one crying in the wilderness, make straight the way of the Lord, as said the prophet Esaias" **(John 1: 22-23).**

The First Attraction

If you're married, think of those days, I mean the first time you sighted your wife or the first thing you saw in your wife that got you attracted to her. Or that makes you fall head over heels in love with her.

What was it? Were you just attracted to her for the sake of attraction? No! There was something more than that, or to that! There was something in her that tickles your fancy when you first saw her, something that knocks you off-balance.

Maybe you were attracted to her because she's always looking radiant and sexy. Or maybe because she doesn't care a pin about you even though she knew you wanted her, and that drove you crazy because you wanted her badly enough within your grasp!

Maybe she represents a melodious song that fascinates you. Maybe she's like a dancing music each time she walks.

Or maybe she has a singularly and fresh eyes, so wonderfully pretty and honest, or if I should go a little bit over the hedge, maybe because of her voluptuous hip and militant breast! Or because she walks like an angel on a fashion parade!

Or maybe her tone was decidedly sociable and flirtatious. Maybe **everything about her was triumphantly elegant.**

However the truth is, whatever **maybe t**he reasons, you were attracted to her, nontheless. She really got you off your rocker or knocks you off your feet! I mean she got into you! That was the first honey that attracted you to her.

So what I'm I trying to say? Very simple: Your Public Ads Is the First Honey That Will Attract Your Audience to Your Speaking Event.

It's a lot easier to catch a fly with honey than vinegar. That is why big companies will continue to make huge money from ordinary day-to-day people who think and thus believe they are poor.

It's quite unfortunate, even though it's a sad truth that poor people make big companies bigger and richer, and thus give them the right to bully them with their product hypes and gimmicks.

Now think of it this way. What do you think most average companies do to make huge profits from the common man? Is it because they give you vinegar in place of water? Maybe!

Or is it because you've known them well enough as a big, successful, and reputable companies that delivers on their terms? Maybe!

Or is it because . . . because . . . because . . . **they offer you honey instead of vinegar?** Yes, yes, and yes!

And that is the reason for their success as they offer it to YOU at a very costly prize! They know what you want! And you often go for it! And you often pay for it! And you often get yourself broke and in debt! And you often make them rich and richer still!

The telecommunication industries are very good at it. So learn from them.

If you must attract the flies to your events you must **learn how to offer honey in**

place of vinegar! So what is the honey? The honey is what they really want from the event you're trying to organize; or the benefits you claim to offer.

Preach Your Claim and Offer What You Preach

Think about when you first met your spouse? Was it honey or vinegar you offer her? Didn't you appreciated and commend on her beauty? Didn't you say all what you could say that was within your grasp?

Didn't you turned into a poet for her sake and for the sake of love and speaks so romantically to her? And each time you checked on her wasn't your voice mild, milky, and supple?

Yes!

So the same is applicable to your speaking business. Offer your target audience the honey, I mean what they really want from the event you want to organize.

For example, they may read from your public poster or flyer, **How To Make $1,500+ Monthly Working from Home.**

What they really want is that $1,500+ without necessarily leaving the comfort of their home. Or to put it this way, without any hassle.

Why?

Because they wants to buy a new sport car and an apartment complex overlooking Aso Rock; they wants to make a show-off with their new fortunes either to their friends and neighbors, put on both intimidating regalia and the latest designer wears to living a shinning lifestyle like that of a superstar!, whatever star there was that has turned super in their eyes.

Now, if you know what they want as they attend your seminar you must know how to skillfully show them the way to your claim.

Thus you must learn and know your audience mindset! **Then with what you know and/or love doing,** offer them the benefits of attending your speaking conference.

Your public ad is the first invitation to your audience. And should have some benefits and inform your audience on what they'll stand to gain by attending your presentation.

Therefore, the need to properly plan your publicity which is very crucial to your success as an integral part of your speaking business can not be overemphasis; and it must contain the theme (or topics to be discuss), time, date, venue (and/or some popular or well known guest speakers in the subject **if any**).

If you feel there are some other people whom you would love to grace the occasion, well, you can as well send them a personal invitation to attend the seminar before the D-day.

Chapter 20: Maintain A Positive Attitude

Apositive attitude can help one to overcome the fear of speaking in public. Harbouring negative thoughts about your situation will only serve to place mental obstacles in your way, undermine your self-confidence and heighten your fears.Maintaining a positive attitude can help you to deal with those negative emotions that cause you to be fearful. So, relax and try not to dwell on unrealistic fears. Instead, focus your energy on ways to deal with your fears. Try to reflect on past successes or focus on ways in which you can make your performance a success. Remember that you are trying to eliminate your fear, not increase it.Use positive affirmations to help clear your mind of negative thoughts about your situation. Here are some affirmations you might find useful when you are feeling fearful: "I am doing a good job", "I know my speech is informative and interesting". "I am going to be a success". I am sure you will have a few positive affirmations of your own. Don't be afraid to use them.So, cultivate and maintain a positive mental attitude throughout to help you to overcome your fear and achieve the success you deserve.

Resources Available

Numerous resources are available to help you overcome any fears you have of speaking in public.Many organisations offer training courses and self-help materials.There are online courses and video to help overcome public speaking anxiety and many agencies offer one to one training in the delivery of a speech.

One United Kingdom based public speaking and communications company is The College of Public Speaking (CoPS).Their training programmes include short workshops, tailor-made programmes for individuals and accredited short courses.One of their aims is to raise awareness of public speaking as an essential social skill. The college offers a

Diploma in Spoken Communication. It is an interactive, open learning qualification, delivered via the Internet. It is open to students worldwide.

Video is an important source of training potential as it reveals actual examples of behaviour to emulate in addition to verbal knowledge transfer.Another option available is to join a public speaking club such as Toastmasters International, Powertalk International or The Society of Cogers, where individuals are taught effective public speaking techniques.

Presentation Tools and Visual Aids

Make use of tools and materials that can assist you in the making your speech.

There are many presentation programs available that a speaker can use, such as Microsoft PowerPoint, OpenOffice.org Impress, Apple Keynote, including modern internet-based presentation programs in Google Docs and SlideRocket. Microsoft PowerPoint is a popular presentation program that runs on Microsoft Windows and Apple's Mac OS X operating system. Of course, there are the older visual aid technologies, such as slides, chalkboards, handouts, pamphlets, flip charts and posters.These can be of benefit to both speaker and audience.A presentation program makes it easier for speakers to access their ideas and provides the audience with visual information, which compliments the speech.

Research conducted by the Wharton School of Business in the United States found that audiences believe presenters who use visual aids are more professional and credible than presenters who merely speak.They also showed that the use of visuals reduced meeting times by 28 percent. In other research conducted, it has been found that meetings and presentations, reinforced with visuals, help participants reach decisions and consensus more quickly.

Chapter 21: Public Speaking Is Easy Communication Is The Key

Communication is the key to your becoming a successful and effective speaker!

What is communication? I asked you in the first chapter to find a definition. This is where that definition comes in handy. You need to be clear in your mind what communication really is so that you can relate to your audience at every level.

You may have written down as a fear, that you fear not getting your audience's attention. It's all about the communication. Before you even begin to analyze your audience, you need to understand yourself as a communicator. Ask yourself some questions like:

DoIhaveclearideasonwhatIwantto share?

Do I wish to share information?

Is it important to share the information that I need to share?

Do I have the knowledge required to share the information?

Only you can answer these questions, but they should point you in the direction of how you need to proceed.

In communication you really want to inform, excite, inspire or motivate your audience.Sometimes you have multiple objectives. But first you must understandandbeclearonwhatyouwantto achieve.Ensure you have at least three good points to share and give examples, tell stories, or illustrate pictures.

As an audience member, think about what would cause you to listen keenly to a speaker for 5 to 20 minutes. That is an indication of what and how you would want to communicate.

Barriers to Communication

Every public speaker will have to deal with barriers to communication. Each public speaker must prepare to break through various barriers that may come up in the process of a speech delivery. Sometimes the fault does not lay with the presenter but audience members may have certain blocks that prevent you from connecting with them. I should just like to mention a few here.

Recently I had a presentation on stress management to staff members in an organization. When I was introduced, you could see by the folded arms, the slouching in the chairs of the staff members, some were even playing on their cell phones, showing that they had little interest in my speech. Immediately, I noted that this was a direct barrier to what I was asked to communicate.This is seen as a psychological barrier; it was clear that they did not want to be in a staff meeting, which is usually mandatory.

How did I overcome?By getting the audience involved by asking questions so that I could get their attention and involvement. This is the strategy I had to use for the majority of the presentation because I could see that these persons were not open to any such information. In the end, I could determine that what I had to share was received by quite a number of persons as the session progressed.

Other barriers to communication include:

Cultural barriers

Physical barriers

Religious barriers

Gender barriers

Technical barriers

Physiological barriers

Cultural barriers

Cultural barriers exist where persons of diverse backgrounds comprise your audience.

Cultural barriers may also exist within an organization, within its hierarchy – the ground staff, the supervisors, middle management and top management.

Audience members may come from different geographical and socio-economic areas, with different life approaches, understandings and life views. You need to be aware of who is really in your audience;

sometimes you may know them well, other times you may not. Do your research.

Physical barriers

Physical barriers may include the area where the presentation may be held; can the audience see and hear the speaker?

That is why it is always important to get a view of where you will be speaking beforehand so that you are prepared. Is the room big or is it small? Is the sound appropriate? You have been in an audience where you may have seen this type of communication barrier at work.

Religious barriers & Gender barriers

These barriers are a subset of cultural barriers.In some scenarios the audience will receive a male speaker better than a female speaker and vice versa.

You must be aware of gender issues when you go to do a presentation, if any such barrier exists.As far as religious barriers are concerned, this is mostly related to the content of your speech.Be careful not to make statements that have the potential to offend, especially if that is not your intention.Again, it is important for you to do your background checks.

Technical barriers

Technical barriers occur where you rely on equipment to support your presentation. Light and power are important; the use of technological equipment must be appropriate to the occasion. Make sure you have all the necessary support to perform your public speaking task well.

Physiological barriers

Never forget that we may have members of varying abilities in your audience.Some audience members may not be able to hear or see due to their personal physical limitations.Makes sure as you prepare your material you take this into consideration.

UNDERSTANDING COMMUNICATION BARRIERS

Once you begin to understand what communication barriers you may face, you begin to release the fear of standing in front of the audience and thinking it is alluptoyou(inawayitis—butjustdoyour research).

Communication is the key to making public speaking easy, be clear, precise and informed — give value for the attention that persons will give you as a speaker. They really are on your side.

Chapter 22: Speak With More Than Your Voice

There is a bit of a misperception about the phrase "public speaking". The misperception that the technique of becoming good at public speaking is all in how you speak. The truth is that your voice is only part of what you need to be successful in giving a presentation to a group of people. To be an effective public 'speaker", you should use every resource you have including your body language, your arms and your legs to capture the attention of the crowd and hold it.

There is nothing more boring than a speaker who stands in one place and never moves his arms and speaks softly just putting out the information of the talk. So to avoid this curse, learn not only to communicate with your entire being when you are in front of an audience. Learn to express yourself with facial expressions, with gestures of your arms and with movement. Because that extra effort is what can make a fair presentation good or a good presentation a great one.

A good public presentation can be compared to eating a meal in a restaurant. A good chef knows that there is more to fine dining than just food because you also must have good service and ambiance so the presentation of the food makes the meal delightful to eat. The same is true of a public speaking situation. It isn't enough just to stand up there and speak out the information. You are not just speaking because you are only really successful when you are communicating. And to communicate, your audience has to grasp what you are saying and be prepared to make it real in their own lives.

Movement is probably the most underused public speaking method but it is also one of the most effective. To put it bluntly, when you speak to a group, don't just stand there. Get out of the podium and move around a bit. Walk from one side of your speaking area to the other. Use your hands to help you describe an illustration or to gesture with emphasis toward the crowd when your text fits that kind of expression. This movement is good for you because it's a way of walking off your nervousness. It's good for the audience because it keeps them interested. And it's very good for your presentation because it is a powerful way to get your point across and to assure you are being understood.

The relationship between public speaking and public performance is unmistakable. When you watch a speaker, the key word is "watch". Taking in the presentation of a speaker is an event that brings in all of the senses. And the more your audience actually "experiences you" rather than just hears what you say, the better they will like your presentation and the more likely they will be to agree with what you have to say or take action in the direction you had hoped they would.

Of course, it can be a nervous moment the first time you decide to step away from the podium and use your body as part of your presentation. If you walk and move in front of people, there is always the chance an accident can happen. You could swing your arms in emphasis and knock something over. You could trip over a microphone cord and be in danger of falling down. Or your wardrobe could malfunction because of the increased stress and that would be a horrible thing to deal with when everyone is looking at you. You can do take some extra measures to be sure your wardrobe is secure beforehand and to evaluate the speaking setting so you are aware of potential causes of accidents. But the possibility of a mishap is just a risk that you should be prepared to take because the movement you use is so powerfully effective that the rewards are too great to pass up.

The other risk is that by stepping away from the podium, you step away from your outline. To enable yourself to wean away from having to have that outline in front of you all the time, select one or two sections where you will depart the outline and share a personal story. Then your movement will be confident and effective. And when you can integrate confident movement into your presentation, your public speaking skills will go from good to great instantaneously.

Professional Speakers Polish Their Message

One key to delivering a successful message is polishing the message you already have. You will find that your audience can better understand what you have to say when you message targets specific key points rather than vague generalities. Since your audience is looking for information that will benefit them, they will need the specifics on how your topic can be used in their lives! Here are some ways to polish the great message you already have!

1. Make it interesting. As simple as this sounds many beginning professional speakers fail to engage their audiences simply because their message is not interesting. This doesn't mean that what they had to say had no value, but rather the message did not inspire anyone to take a sincere interest.

2. Stay on track. Even the best professional speakers can get off track in their delivery. This adds confusion to the basic message they were trying to communicate and could hinder anyone receiving the message at all.

3. Make your message clear and concise. You can overload your audience with detailed facts. While you do want to be precise and give accurate information, too much information will literally boggle their minds! If you have a lot of details that you want them to have, use a separate handout and refer to that. Doing so will make it easier on your audience to digest the wonderful news you have to share.

4. Make your message effective. Do you have a goal with your presentation? What actions do you want your audience members to take once they are done hearing you? Your presentation should lead your audience down a path to take action on the things you want them to do. Consider yourself to be a tour guide leading them to key highlights of information within your presentation. Your presentation should always conclude with an action step whether it means taking a test or buying reference products and materials.

5. Make your message personal. While you speak to a group of people, your message is tailored to each and every single person in your audience. You can connect with them individually by relaying personal situations they might find themselves in. You can connect with them by bringing in the emotional aspect (i.e. - fear, inspiration, dreams) into your presentation. The bottom line of your

presentation is to connect with your audience one on one while addressing the entire group.

6. Check the "political correctness" of your message. You can lose or offend your audience if you don't pay attention to the political correctness of your message. Talking about sensitive subjects like money, culture, and even type of language used requires you to exert sensitivity concerning your audience.

Delivering the best message comes with the diligent attention and care to the details of your presentation. Take time to refine and hone your message so that you can have confidence that you've presented your information well and on target. Be specific about what you say and engage your audience to ensure that you are the answer to their problems! Professional speakers take the time to polish their message!

Successful Transitions For Your Presentation

Having a smoothly flowing presentation relies on having successful transitions as you proceed from point to point. Even your transitions do need some level of planning. As your audience processes the information you present in their minds, jerky transitions become hard to follow and comprehend. You could potentially lose your audience in a transition without even realizing it and by the time they catch up to you, they'll have missed 2/3 of the next point you're trying to make. Here are some examples you can easily implement into your presentation to make it a success!

- Use bridge words or phrases. These are words like "finally", "however", "in addition", 'moreover" and 'meanwhile". This bridge helps your audience to stay connected with your message. These words or phrases represent linkages between the points you make.
- Use the same word or idea twice. You can say, "A similar idea is that..." or 'this is

what people see... this is what people think...".

- Ask a question. Engage your audience and emphasize the points you are trying to make. "Was there ever a time when..." "How many of you..."

- Refer back to information previously stated in your presentation. "Remember when I told you earlier..."

- Review the points you'll be making or the point you've made. Itemize them one by one. You can say, "There are 5 important concepts to know..."

- Use a visual. Use a prop to finalize your point or even introduce the next point you are going to make. Insert a humorous cartoon or image for your audience to focus on.

- Use a pause. Give your audience a moment to think about what you just said. You can also introduce a dramatic pause for evoking emotions.

- Use physical movement or a change in the tone of your voice. Walk to different parts of the stage. Use different gestures or postures to emphasize what you mean. Change your tone of voice as you are speaking.

- Use testimonials or a personal story. Let your audience know what other people are saying about what you're talking about. Make your points more relatable by telling your audience how you or someone else handled the issue or problem.

One of the most common mistakes that professional speakers make is that they don't use transitions in their presentation. You could potentially lose your audience because they aren't processing your information as quickly as you want them to. Another common mistake is that the transitions used are too short. Transitions are processing times for your audience. It gives them a chance to catch up to where you are at in delivering your message. The last most common mistake made with using transitions are that the same transition is used over and over again in a presentation. Vary your transitions and your presentation become more interesting.

While only representing a small portion of your presentation, transitions are powerful tools you can use to keep your audience tuned in to what you have to say. If you're not seeing the success you'd like to see with your audience, consider working on improving your transitions.

Chapter 23: How To Give A Dynamic Introduction

Your introduction sets to tone for the rest of your speech. So, you can appreciate how important it is to get it right within the first few minutes of speaking. Before you utter a single word, the first thing you need to do is, pay attention to your appearance. Remember, one of the five pillars of effective public speaking talks about public perception. You need to use your outfit to send a clear message, without distractingyour audience, of course. Rather, the outfit should be put together in such a way that their focus remains on you. This is the first part of creating a dynamic introduction. So, we will start off with that.

1. Look the Part

Unless you have a very strong point to make, wearing a garish outfit on stage can end up taking the attention of your audience from what you want to say. Dressing the part doesn't mean that you have to grab the first outfit from the runway. It means coordinating yourself in a way that shares the same narrative with what you are about to say. For professional events, simplicity is usually the best. A nice, well iron shirt combined with straightened out pants and formal shoes should do the trick. If you really want to keep it formal, throw on a nice blazer. For a semi casual look, do what most professionals do. Trade your formal pants for khakis or jeans. Wear nice, comfortable shoes in colors that are either neutral or nude and keep the rest of the outfit within the professional family. No excessive jewelry, no outlandish colors and definitely excessive use of patterns and graphics.

2. Start Off with Niceties

When you meet someone new for the first time, courtesy demands that you introduce yourself. Talk to them about who you are for a few seconds (if you were not introduced). And since you cannot go around the whole audience asking everyone to introduce themselves, acknowledge them by giving them a compliment. Make a genuine statement about how nice they look today or infuse a little joke about how they are stern faces might be intimidating you and perhaps jokingly asked the audience to be nice on you today. This might not get a full belly roll laughter but it gets it gets the smiles going. And that always lifts the mood in any room.

3. Go Futuristic

If you are an avid movie lover, you would know that in an interesting movie, directors have this technique where the movie plays out a futuristic event in the opening scene before bringing it back to the present. And then the rest of the movie walks you through the series of incidences that occurs and leads you to that futuristic point that got you all hot and bothered in the first place. This method builds interests from the second you start watching. Employ the same technique by asking your audience questions that will frame a desired possible future in their minds. The questions that you ask should be able to draw up a picture that is vivid in the minds of your audience.With this image the forefront, you can now walk them through this journey with the rest of your talk.

This is just one way to ensure that you are able to grab the attention of your audience from the second you get on stage. There are different introduction techniques. You just have to find the one that works for you.

Task:

your assignment today is to go online and look for your favourite public speakers on YouTube. You will find a lot of them on TED talk events. Pay attention to the first 5 minutes of their speech. What are the things you noticed? List them out and then see how you can incorporate these techniques in your own presentation.

Chapter 24: Informative Speaking

Many students are concerned about designing a purely informative speech for their audience. Speakers wanting to be successful with this type of presentation must avoid unwittingly creating a persuasive speech. This guide sheet will give you a better understanding of the characteristics of an informative speech.

Informative speaking can be loosely defined as sharing knowledge and reducing audience ignorance. Speeches of this type likely describe an activity, event, object person, or place, demonstrate an event or activity, or explain abstract or complicated subjects or issues. Here are some general tips to help speakers write informative speeches:

1. Imagine you are an anchor on National Public Radio news, or a trainer for your

job. It is the job of these individuals to inform listeners of new topics. Another analogy is when a friend comes to a movie late and you have to tell them what has already happened. This is an example of an informative speech; you (the speaker) have no bias and no reason to persuade your friend (the audience) one way or another. This is your task for an informative presentation—you are informing them without inserting your own opinion.

2. Avoid imparting your personal bias on your audience. While this is difficult, if your speech topic is controversial, it is still possible to present an impartial presentation of the ideas.

3. Choose a topic that you are not too passionate about. For example, if you spent the last four years of your life being an ardent supporter of the death penalty then it may be too difficult to present the opposing perspective in an

unbiased manner. The issue of abortion is also a very controversial topic. A person who volunteered their time to a pro-choice campaign—although knowledgeable
on the subject—may be unable to equally and fairly represent the
pro-life side of the debate.

4. Focus on quality, non-opinionated research for all sides of the issue. If a
speaker cites highly credible information for one side of an issue and then
cites questionable or unreliable evidence for another, listeners will perceive
the speaker's bias toward the topic. Speakers should be constantly cognizant
of the quality of evidence to which they refer. This is especially important
when the desire is to fairly represent all sides of an issue.

While informative speeches are designed to describe, demonstrate, or explain
issues, persuasive speeches are designed to move listeners to act or

adopt a perspective. Concerned informative speakers will evaluate their presentations for these signs of persuasive speaking. For example, a speech that informs listeners about the debate on gay marriage will explain the status quo and possibly alternative views of the issue. A persuasive speech on the other hand will attempt to change listeners' mind. A speaker has done her or his job well if, at the end of the speech, listeners are able to form their own opinion on the topic, while at the same time not necessarily knowing what position the speaker holds.

Chapter 25: Sharpshooters And Hecklers

Here is a subject I feel is one of the main contributors to why people have a fear of public speaking. You will, without a doubt, have a bout with a sharpshooter and heckler in your speaking career. This will happen more than once. Count on it! You need to arm yourself with the tools on how to handle these types of people. We are going to try and understand why sharpshooters and hecklers exist.

Let's take a look at the Sharpshooter. These are people whose game is to take a verbal shot at you for their own personal agenda. These are the people who classify themselves as the "Know-it-All" experts in everything, regardless of the subject. They will even do research on the subject matter you will be presenting to try and catch you off-guard and take the shot. Their goal is to discredit you and place the focus on them as an expert. In most cases these people are very calculating and know when to take the shot.

This is a control tactic to set themselves apart from others. They place the spotlight on them and away from the presenter to make them look good in the eyes of their management, constituents and co-workers. There is nothing wrong with wanting to look good to one's management, especially if they are vying for a promotion or a new opportunity. The unfortunate thing about sharpshooters is that they choose to. **Sharpshooters can be and are very dangerous. If they are successful, your credibility will suffer.**

Compared to sharpshooter, hecklers are playing a game. Their goal is normally to liven up what they think is a somewhat uninteresting presentation, or just to "have some fun" with you, they will ask you questions that are rather difficult, if not impossible, to answer. They want to see if they can knock you off balance and subject or get you off on a tangent. They will often try to entrap you in your own logic. They will also interject unsolicited humor. The heckler isn't as concerned with your reply as with making the meeting more interesting and having some "fun" with you and of course placing the spotlight on themselves for a moment. This is a sport to the heckler. However, the Sharpshooter might pose the identical question stated by the heckler, but, for a more serious purpose. They believe they can do this either by discrediting you or by saying something more brilliant than anything you've said. The calculating sharpshooter will not use humor in their tactic. Knowing this will help you in determining how to handle the situation.

Scanning your audience before your presentation will not reveal a sharpshooter, if there is one. They are too cunning to tip their hat. You might be able to determine a potential heckler by scanning the audience before your speech. What you look for here is a person who is acting like a clown with the people in close proximity. Things like loud laughter and jovial interaction are usually, but, not always, indications of a heckler. You can gather information about your audience if a speaker precedes you. Sharpshooters and hecklers usually aren't fussy about who they attack. You can often see who may be a problem by paying close attention to audience comments and questions directed to the speaker before you. If you're the only speaker to a group of people you don't know, it is advisable to ask someone familiar with attendees whether he or she knows of anyone in the group who might give you a challenge. Known sharpshooters and hecklers usually have reputations that precede them and having that knowledge is invaluable.

Dealing with Sharpshooters and Hecklers

There are ways to successfully handle sharpshooters and hecklers and maintain credibility. Being prepared for them is by far the most important. In your pre-preparation a week or so before your event, there are a couple of things you can do. If you have to present statistical data, know it cold and bring the hard copy, or place it in electronically in your presentation as reference. Also, ask yourself the question; "What is the worst question I could get on this subject?" **Know your subject well. If you have a weak spot in your presentation, shore it up!**

Here is an example: Say a person states that your statistical data is wrong. How do you address a potential damaging comment like that? First, show no emotion of any kind. If any, show
 inquisitiveness and posture yourself as questioning. Then ask, "please show me where" and present your statistical backup data to the person making the attack. If you wish to defuse, you can ask in a humorous manner and posture like; "please show me the error of my ways!" Again, present your statistical backup data. There are normally only two results here. One, you have proven your information is correct and your attacker probably won't bother you again. Or, two, your attacker was right and "You are toast!" Yes, you can make an apology, but your credibility is shot, at least for this presentation.

If you have diffused this situation and provided creditable statistical data, by doing your homework, your credibility just went off the charts. And for your sharpshooter? You won't hear from that person the rest of the presentation. Normally, if this attack was planned and failed, your attacker will silently slide out the door. You might not see it happen, but, your audience will. Regardless if you see it or not, pay no attention and continue your presentation as nothing happened.

If someone attacks you in a general statement, insist that this person be specific, such as, "Could you please give me a specific example?" Focus on specifics, rather than generalities. Often, sharpshooters throw out comments without much forethought and are simply trying to position themselves publicly with their specific agenda.

Never look upset or show you are rattled. To a sharpshooter, that's like throwing chum into a shark frenzy. Remember, sometimes their goal is just to irritate or knock you off stride. If this happens you could become too anxious to answer in a clear, rational way. Also, you're likely to lose your train of thought for the balance of the presentation. Maintain composure at all times.

How do you keep from looking upset? As soon as the first three words are out of your
 sharpshooter's mouth, do an immediate, silent check of your facial muscles. Make a conscious effort to relax these muscles. When this happens to me, I smirk. I can't help it! I know when that smirk appears…it's on! You may not feel like smiling, but attempt to look relaxed and welcoming. Relax the rest of your body as well. Be sure you're not standing rigid or with both hands on your hips. Oh, and your eyes, now this is hard to do, but don't "shoot daggers" from your eyes when the sharpshooter takes the shot! The first thing that should pop into your mind is, be cool! Say you're presenting to 100 people

in an auditorium. Understand when you are in front of people your senses are heightened. You are so focused on giving a great presentation, the smallest sound can be heard from across the room. **Then it happens, the sharpshooter takes the shot. Trust me; you will hear 198 eyeballs "click" right on to you.**

Your audience is now going to watch you very carefully to see how you're going to address this. If you suddenly appear, through body language, to be alarmed or fearful of the sharpshooter, your audience might think you have reason to be. You never give your audience that impression, not even a hint.

Don't blow off your sharpshooter or not deal with the comment. **It's like the Piranha Theory; if one feeds, they all will feed. Don't set yourself up as lunch!** If you blow off your sharpshooter or heckler, it may be perceived by the heckler or sharpshooter and your audience as an evasion. Sharpshooters often have a special kind of courage to ask the tough question that might be running through everyone's mind. Whereas, the others may be too shy or too polite to ask. A sharpshooter will take the shot! If your sharpshooter's question is a good one, you owe everyone an answer.

In answering, apply the "Duck in the Pond" theory; you may look calm on the surface, but your feet are paddling like heck under the surface. Answer calmly and politely, never confrontationally. If you've did your pre-prep (Chapter 5), this should be a walk in the park Also, imagining the worst questions and practicing your answers to them beforehand is certainly helpful. The real test will be in the moment of the sharpshooters shot. Your heart starts to pound, blood pressure rises, you feel your adrenalin kick in. This is the test! It doesn't get more fun than this. It's on! **"Okay, okay, hold on, relax, gee I'm getting excited here!"** You are in the thick of it!

Maintain your composure as you are the expert and the professional here just diffuse the situation, address the issue and go on. **Personally; I like a sharpshooter now and then. Its fun! Keeps me sharp!**

Remember, your audience is watching you very closely. They will remember how you handled the situation. If you get defensive, visibly tense, or argumentative your audience may think you're scared of your sharpshooter or maybe hiding something. If, in anger, you attempt to take out your opponent, your audience may begin to fear you. They may even see you as merciless. If they fear you, they most likely won't support you in other situations. After all, when might you mercilessly turn on them in the same way? Don't risk losing their support and respect over one sharpshooter.

It's really easy to take a defensive attitude when someone is publicly attacking us in their attempts discredit, or trying to play games. Isn't it okay to show anger in this situation? The answer here is…NO! It may not be fair, but, there's no law against what your sharpshooter or heckler is doing. You might not like it, but, visibly showing your anger will not help you.

Successful professionals remain in control. Train yourself to look at issues and data and keep personalities out of the venue. Many in your audience will, no doubt, secretly envy your ability to remain calm, fearing that they wouldn't be able to do as well if in your shoes. Some may even personally compliment you afterward for "keeping your cool."

Let's take a minute and talk about an attack word. The word "you" is a personal attack word. When used in a crucial conservation it can and most likely will agitate your adversary. When formulating your response to your sharpshooter or heckler try not to use the word "you." This may be difficult if you are in the heat of the moment. First you must be sure your information is correct. So let the sharpshooter present his/her case. Here is an example of what I'm talking about: You reply, "You are stating that the statistics presented are incorrect. Would you please substantiate this? This example is an attack, without question. You have painted your sharpshooter in the corner and this may be what you wanted to do, but, you really can't. Now using the same example, what is a better way to say the same thing? "Let's take a quick moment to look at this, if the audience doesn't mind, **(pause here and take a look at the audience for acceptance)** as I don't wish to present erroneous information." You now present the correct information directly in a very polite and professional manner to the audience and the sharpshooter and politely ask if all is understood. Okay now what happened here? This tactic accomplishes two things. One, the sharpshooter has to expose themselves to the audience and must present substantiation for the "shot," which will be discredited. And two, you will gain the respect of your audience and silence your sharpshooter. This was a nonaggressive, non-confrontational response, which in reality discredited your attacker and at the same time "you took them out"! So, in formulating your response, try to avoid the use of the word "you."

If possible, be so thoroughly familiar with your material that you have the answer in your head. If you want to show some backup figures, have those ready on an overhead presentation close by. Explain your logic as best you can, looking calm, relaxed, and maintaining eye contact. You may even want to move slightly closer to your opponent as you speak. Assertive body language transmits confidence. **This is where you go into the stealth mode. Line up your target and return fire. Get the focus off you and on to your attacker, Remember, never be confrontational, and just be right!**

Keep your comment or answer short. Don't dwell on the discussion. Once you have responded to the sharpshooter, accept, maybe one more comment. Then, make one more brief response yourself, if required. If your opponent still won't let go, state that you'd be happy to address this in a more detailed manner personally after the presentation. Now here is a cool way to reset the atmosphere. Thank the sharpshooter for their comments and if you had asked their name at the time of the initial shot, use it in your gratitude statement.

Let's say you've successfully handled your heckler's or sharpshooter's comment. You had your answer ready and spoke calmly, with good eye contact and self-assurance. You now continue on with your presentation. Is your sharpshooter finished with you? Don't bet on it.

After an initial confrontation with a heckler or sharpshooter, many public speakers will make the mistake of purposely avoiding eye contact with the now exposed sharpshooter or heckler for the remainder of the presentation, in hopes of avoiding another shot. The heckler or sharpshooter wants attention. If you proceed as if they aren't there, they will be more likely to remind you of their presence. Even if you continue to provide good eye contact, they still may not let you off the hook. There may be a round 2 coming.

You have an additional advantage at this point that you didn't have before your first run-in. You now know who your heckler or sharpshooter is. If there are more you don't know about and you handled the first well you might not get another taker. Regardless you've been through one with success, so you can do it again.

What if you're caught off guard or outgunned? Let's assume you didn't do very well in round one. Your heckler or sharpshooter rattled you. You got nervous, defensive, and didn't respond with a very effective answer. Don't be disappointed in yourself. It takes skill and practice to have a successful exchange with people who are out to get you. But, don't give up. Sharpshooters and hecklers are a fact in the public speaking world. If you're at the beginning or in the middle of your presentation, you'll certainly get a second chance to try again. Hecklers and sharpshooters usually don't limit themselves to one shot or comment.

If you know what you did wrong in the first round, you will be better prepared should there be a second round. However, if your sharpshooter rattled you with a shot like a well landed right hook, you may feel lucky just to get through the rest of your presentation and out of the "ring" in one piece. And you know, that's okay.

Always have a failsafe. What I mean by that is that you must always be prepared for the unexpected. Have a meeting prior to your presentation with the event coordinator find out who the security guards are, or even if there are any. In this meeting you want to establish a signal for and out of control attendee. Now this may not be a heckler or sharpshooter, but it might be someone who has become ill or maybe had a little bit too much to drink. Establish a subtle signal that you can send to the officials or coordinators standing back of the room. This signal is used only for the purpose of removing a person from the venue. Again, this is absolutely a last resort. However, don't forget to set this up prior to the presentation.

Afterward, critique yourself on how you handled the situation with the sharpshooter and what you did or said that gave them the advantage. Preferably, ask another audience member, soon after your presentation, what you could have done differently. Continue to sharpen your skills in this area. Understand these people are trying to publicly prevent your success. Whether you become successful quickly in dealing with problem people, or whether it takes some time to feel confident in these situations, it is important to remember the certain things we've discussed in this chapter. Pre-preparation is critical. Know your subject and be prepared mentally to handle what comes your way. Be cool, calm and collected. Always treat your adversary with courtesy and respect. Finally, never, ever, loose your cool or show fear. Maintain total professionalism and understand they're always out there, lurking. Just be ready!

Conclusion

You have now learned some very important secrets to public speaking. If you will use them, you will speak well and effectively. If you choose short cuts and try to make your audience think you know something you don't, they will figure you out. I encourage you to communicate with integrity and do your best. Your audience's ears and minds are waiting for what you have to say!

www.ingramcontent.com/pod-product-compliance
Lightning Source LLC
Chambersburg PA
CBHW072002070526
44583CB00015B/1290